Seeking the God Beyond

Seeking the God Beyond

A Beginner's Guide to
Christian Apophatic Spirituality

J. P. Williams

CASCADE *Books* · Eugene, Oregon

SEEKING THE GOD BEYOND
A Beginner's Guide to Christian Apophatic Spirituality

Copyright © 2019 Janet P. Williams. All rights reserved. Except for brief quotations in critical publications or reviews, no part of this book may be reproduced in any manner without prior written permission from the publisher. Write: Permissions, Wipf and Stock Publishers, 199 W. 8th Ave., Suite 3, Eugene, OR 97401.

Originally published in the UK under the title *Seeking the God Beyond* by SCM Press, 2018.

Cascade Books
An Imprint of Wipf and Stock Publishers
199 W. 8th Ave., Suite 3
Eugene, OR 97401

www.wipfandstock.com

PAPERBACK ISBN: 978-1-5326-8576-7
HARDCOVER ISBN: 978-1-5326-8577-4
EBOOK ISBN: 978-1-5326-8578-1

Cataloguing-in-Publication data:

Names: Williams, Janet P., author.

Title: Seeking the God beyond : a beginner's guide to Christian apophatic spirituality / J. P. Williams.

Description: Eugene, OR: Cascade Books, 2019

Identifiers: ISBN 978-1-5326-8576-7 (paperback) | ISBN 978-1-5326-8577-4 (hardcover) | ISBN 978-1-5326-8578-1 (ebook)

Subjects: LCSH: Negative theology—Christianity. | Spirituality. | Asceticism. | Mysticism.

Classification: BV5032 W45 2019 (print) | BV5032 (ebook)

Manufactured in the U.S.A.

Contents

Truly, you are a God who hides himself,

O God of Israel, the Saviour.

Isaiah 45.15

About the Artist

Carole Bury is a contemporary textile artist whose practice utilizes much loved drawing and adept stitching skills.

She purposefully and patiently explores themes concerned with her love of nature and the world about her, economically paring down details until only an essence of the original is present.

As my pencils and charcoal dance and skitter over the paper I sense I am guided to release the secrets of myself and those of my subject. Drawing is an internal dialogue, a conversation between artist and nature, during which each small detail is discussed. At its very core, my drawing is an invitation to the viewer to 'listen in'.

Carole lives and works high up in the Cotswolds in a small village. On her doorstep is an expansive, inspirational landscape, rich in source material – the perfect environment for striding out and feeding the soul and body.

Preface

You might think of this as the theological equivalent of a book about wild-swimming. It isn't either a how-to manual for novice swimmers, or a serious book of instruction for those who want to become Olympic achievers. It isn't aiming to convince you that wild-swimming/apophatic Christianity is worth doing because it will help you achieve something good (whether that is in terms of getting fit or becoming holier). Rather, think of it as a basic exploration of something wonderful that many of us have heard stories about but few have tried. My aim is to say something about what it's like, share some of the time-honoured stories, point out some of the activities that are involved, suggest some places you might go to give it a try. My hope is that I might make it sound delightful enough to tempt you into the water. Just as with a book about wild-swimming, though, there are some caveats. If you're a complete beginner at swimming, you might want to spend some time in the swimming baths with an instructor first, or else make sure you don't go wild-swimming alone, and don't get out of your depth until you're strong enough. Occasionally, someone drowns. If you are wise, though, you may find you have the time of your life.

From a different perspective (although it is in truth about stripping off our 'kit' and diving into the great and wild divine flow), this is about something as far removed from wild-swimming as it is possible to be. The apophatic tradition, which I believe is at the heart of mystical Christianity, is increasingly being recognized not as a joyous hobby for a few but as deeply necessary if the human heart is going to thrive. To put it simply, it is a spiritual discipline for learning to see what's real; it is about finding God, and becoming ourselves.

I spent a long time evading the writing of this, partly bearing in mind the admonition of Ecclesiastes 12.12, that 'Of making many books there is no end, and much study is a weariness of the flesh' and partly because there are already so many fine scholarly books on the apophatic tradition. However, I found that the introductory materials I was sharing with study groups didn't quite sit within an easily available set of covers, so with the generous encouragement of colleagues at Ripon College Cuddesdon, and the fiery questioning hearts of those training for lay and ordained Anglican ministry at the West of England Ministerial Training Course urging me on, I have tried to set out the basic character of this remarkable tradition, indicating something of its importance and the sheer exhilaration of the spiritual ride it offers. Greater minds than mine have said this, so I am in good company and confident to confess that at the worst of times these can seem to be the only wells that still offer sweet living water. Without the apophatic understanding of the way of Christ, I might have got lost. Or, to mangle the wild-swimming metaphor: you might just find a lifebelt in these pages.

The illustrations in this book are kindly provided by Carole Bury, for whose friendship and generous collaboration I am profoundly grateful. Her images speak for themselves. Thanks are due also to the kindly critical friends who offered feedback on earlier versions of this work – to Simon Monk, Karen and Ian Spencer, Mike Eido Luetchford and Hugh Dickinson.

J. P. W.
Cuddesdon, 2018

Introduction

Speak of Me as I Am

There are various names for the spiritual path we're about to explore. It is sometimes known by a Latin name, the *via negativa* or 'negative way'. That can be misleading, as I'll explain below. Sometimes it might be what people mean by 'mystic spirituality' or 'contemplative spirituality', but those can be very broad categories indeed, and within them there are even particular 'brands' of spirituality associated with specific teachers or schools of thought, such as the various contemporary forms of Mindfulness. In some texts and contexts it might be named simply 'prayer' or 'pure prayer' – though unless you're already sensitized to what is meant, this doesn't help. Even though I'll try to avoid jargon as much as possible in what follows, I'm going to use the Greek word for this type of spirituality because I can't find a better one – none of the possible English translations quite capture it. So welcome to this introduction to *apophatic* spirituality in the Christian tradition. If you have already made the acquaintance of this tradition and are reading this book to find out a little more, you may want to skip past the explanation that follows and jump straight to Part 1.

The plot of Shakespeare's *Othello* turns on a profound truth about human psychology. The play opens on to the middle of a conversation: two gentlemen are discussing an unnamed 'him' – the title of the play is our only clue at first as to who 'he' might be. We hear that 'he' is proud and bombastic, self-centred, a Moor with 'thick lips'. We are told that he has 'stolen' (and married) a local young woman (there are uncouth comments about sexuality – he is 'an old black ram'; 'lascivious'); but also that he is a military leader, deemed indispensable.

We don't meet the play's hero, 'the Moor', until Scene 2. (He is not called by his name, Othello, until Scene 3.) Having heard all we have about him it is quite a shock to hear him speak – with restraint, delicacy and some of the play's most poetic lines. Some of the earlier information about him was indeed true – he is a mature man of middle age, Moorish, a warrior and recently married. But the reality of his character when we see him for ourselves is poles apart from the reputation so busily being established in Scene 1. It is clear that the reports given out about Othello tell us a great deal more about prejudice, stereotyping and the character of the speakers than they do about their supposed subject.

The tragedy that follows spins with ghastly inevitability out of this basic theme: how easily we believe what we are told; how often we allow it to blind us to the reality under our noses; how we smash up love and life because we can't shake off the reports other people feed to us, and trust instead to experience and to our own heart's intuition. Othello's heartfelt plea before taking his own life is simple, dignified: 'Speak of me as I am.'

This is a good – albeit anachronistic – starting point for our exploration of apophatic theology. Like the characters in *Othello*, we tend to encounter God's reputation before we (knowingly) encounter God. We gather all sorts of bits and pieces of information about God, some of it good and useful, some of it wildly off-centre and frankly harmful to us and others. Whatever it is we've learned, we need to be sure that when the divine hero strides on to our personal or ecclesial stage, we'll be able to hold it all lightly enough that it won't distort our encounter, won't blind us to any of it, won't influence us to misinterpret it. Hold it lightly enough that we can see what needs to be discarded as rank untruth, and what tells us more about prejudice, stereotype and the character of the speakers than it does about God. The analogy only goes so far, of course. But anything more than a cursory glance at the history of the Christian Church will force us to admit that there is much to make us cry out, with the play's closing lines, that there is much 'tragic loading' in our talk of God, 'more fell than anguish, hunger, or the sea!'.

If we are to speak of God as he is, then, we need to check what we say as often as possible against the touchstone of our experience of living towards holy encounter. And acknowledging that both our individual experiences and accounts of the common experience of the Church can be bent out of shape by prejudice, stereotype and idiosyncrasy, we need always to hold what we say and hear with a certain provisionality. Though this worries many people, there is no contradiction between this and faith: it is Jesus, the 'Way, the Truth and the Life', to whom we are called to be faithful, not a particular interpretation of a set of words. As is often said, the opposite of faith is not doubt but certainty.

From many directions, from the Bible and from philosophy and from the Church's practical experience of prayer as understood down the ages and wrangled into shape by the theologians, there is agreement: God, who reaches out to us in love and mercy, through the life of Jesus Christ and the inspiration of the Holy Spirit, who meets us in worship and sacrament and prayer and in moments of grace in the natural world and in human relationships, is at the same time far beyond our reach. The words we use to describe God are more like gestures to point our attention in the right direction than they are like a scientific description or dictionary definition. God in Godself is beyond not just our language but our minds. We, who stand under God, don't have the kind of perspective that would allow us to understand God.

In the Bible, this is the point made in the last chapters of the book of Job, with their cut-us-down-to-size questions:

'Where were you when I laid the foundation of the earth?
    Tell me, if you have understanding.
Who determined its measurements – surely you know!
    Or who stretched the line upon it?
On what were its bases sunk,
    or who laid its cornerstone,
when the morning stars sang together
    and all the sons of God shouted for joy? (38.4–7)

It is the point made in Isaiah 55.8–9

> For my thoughts are not your thoughts,
>   neither are your ways my ways, declares the LORD.
> For as the heavens are higher than the earth,
>   so are my ways higher than your ways
>   and my thoughts than your thoughts.

We can see Paul's contrast (1 Corinthians 1) between the wisdom of the world and the foolishness of God as a variation on the same theme.

In philosophy, the famous definition of God postulated by the Ontological Argument – by Anselm, Descartes and others – is 'that than which nothing greater can be thought'. This implies, of course, that we can't 'think God' too precisely, because if we could, there would always be a little bit more we could add to think of a greater one. It's an unusual definition, one that ironically makes for a lack of clarity.

In logic, the 'law of non-contradiction' holds that a statement and its contradictory statement cannot both be true of the same object at the same time. This principle is absolutely crucial to honest speech. (It doesn't apply, of course, to poetry and other types of metaphorical language, which have a deeper understanding of honesty and truth.) But it applies only to finite things and beings; it breaks down once we get into the territory of the infinite. Once you notice this, you can immediately see that you won't be able to hang on to statements about God with the same kind of assurance with which you can hang on to statements about material objects or natural laws.

In the same way, if you think about individual words and how we know what they mean, you'll see that they work by dividing reality up into identifiable bits. Definitions enable us to home in on the right bit of reality – so that we can distinguish between a chair and a bed, for example, or between nutritious plants and poisonous ones. Words are a little bit like the machines that slice salami: they cut up reality into digestible chunks. But God isn't a 'bit of reality'. God is the source of the whole thing. So it's not surprising that words won't quite work properly when it comes to God.

In theology, the (almost) unanimous conclusion of the theologians is summed up in St Augustine's memorable phrase: 'If you can understand it, it isn't God'.[1] This doesn't mean that trying to understand God is a waste of time, of course. The whole biblical theme of Wisdom, in the books of Job, Psalms, Proverbs, Ecclesiastes, the Song of Songs (and more if you count the books of the Apocrypha), and the repeated call for us to 'have eyes to see, and ears to hear', indicate otherwise. In particular, we are offered words that are accommodated to our capacity, words derived from the incarnation of the Word as Jesus of Nazareth. But we're not operating on a sort of binary scale, always stuck in 'not understanding' because the only alternative is 'understanding' and that's simply not possible. The point is that there is a whole journey for us to take towards understanding, a journey of increasing maturity. Paul talks about making the transition from baby-milk to solids (1 Corinthians 3.2), and famously about the difference between seeing a distorted image in the sort of polished metal that served the ancient world for a mirror, and seeing clearly, face-to-face (1 Corinthians 13.12). We spend our lives, like the Israelites wandering in the desert, on this journey towards divine truth. Anselm famously called it 'faith seeking understanding'.

We want to speak of God as he is; we know too that our words and ideas tend to become wobbly and unreliable when we point them at the divine. So far, so good: pretty well everyone will agree with this. We haven't got to apophasis yet. In fact all of this could be summed up by adding a footnote to every page of theology, even every page of the Bible: 'Be careful! Taking this *too* literally will damage your spiritual health.' The trouble with all such health warnings is that we can quickly get to the point where we pay them lip-service only. We can just carry on with our Bible readings and our hymns and prayers, our sermons, Christian books and doctrinal statements, looking up at appropriate points to repeat the refrain 'Of course, we must remember that this doesn't entirely capture God . . .'

The apophatic tradition begins from the point at which we pay serious attention to the possibility that there is something much more important than a health warning here. What if it was exactly at the point at which the words go wobbly, at which they start to slip through our fingers, that we might find ourselves able to take an unobstructed glimpse into holy truth? What if it was exactly at the point at which we consent to set aside what we've heard about God that we are best equipped to see clearly the character of the God we encounter? What if the setting-aside turned out to be not a pious footnote but the single most important thing we need to do?

This is the possibility canvassed in some memorable lines of the sixteenth-century Spanish spiritual teacher St John of the Cross. John would sketch for his disciples a little one-page summary diagram of the journey towards encounter with God, using the image of a mountain ascent. Paths lead upward, full of invitation and promise: as the soul draws closer to God, it will be granted possession of the sweet things of earth and heaven, such as joy, consolation and knowledge. But these paths go only so far: they stop short of the summit. The goods they offer are truly good, but that is the problem. They stir up desire in us, and now we seek God no longer for Godself but for ourselves. The true path to the summit is steep and direct; only by stripping ourselves of all such baggage, all ambitions to gain something or even everything, can we attain the summit of glory. John revels in the paradox that to gain all we must desire nothing:

> When you turn toward something
>   you cease to cast yourself upon the all.
> For to go from all to the all
>   you must deny yourself of all in all.
> And when you come to possession of the all
>   you must possess it without wanting anything.
> Because if you desire to have something in all
>   your treasure in God is not purely your all.[2]

Phasis is the ancient Greek word for speech, for talking. In modern English you may have encountered the medical word 'aphasia', signifying the loss of the brain functions that govern speech – it is an effect of brain tumours, for example. If you combine *phasis* with *apo*, which is a preposition meaning 'away from', you get the noun *apophasis* and its adjective form *apophatic*. So apophasis is a practice of going in a certain direction: away from speech.

One way of going away from speech is through denial. We take away whatever's been said by saying 'no' to it. Another way is through saying less and less, disentangling ourselves from the webs of words that usually hold us, gradually falling silent, or making our meaning clear by other means such as gestures. Another way is to use language that undoes itself or points attention away from itself: there is a whole range of possibilities here, including the use of contradiction, paradox, parable and poetry. One type of language that most obviously points away from itself is constituted by words in negative form, starting with a- (like aphasia), in-/im- or un-. So, for example, God is described as *im*mortal, *in*visible, *in*accessible, *un*known. These words work by starting with a familiar meaning ('mortal', 'visible' and so on) and then pointing away from them, in the opposite direction.

Apophatic spirituality can quite often be marked by the use of such words and by similar negative phrases, such as 'God is not . . .', so it can seem appropriate to call it 'negative theology', the *via negativa* ('negative way'). It's unfortunate that this makes it sound less than life-giving! It would hardly be a rich spiritual diet, to dine exclusively on negations.

But this isn't the main reason why the label 'negative theology' doesn't really do justice to apophasis. Negative words and phrases are just the opposite of positive words and phrases (which are generally much more constructive as regards Christian worship and discipleship). Reverting to our salami-slicing analogy for a moment, if a positive word like 'mortal' points to a particular kind of reality, the negative word 'immortal' points to all the other bits of reality. It works by excluding anything that is mortal. When we talk about divinity, though, we're not trying to exclude a set of things and point to what's left over: we're trying to talk about what is beyond all things. We're not pointing to *anything*, really, but to the source of all things.

It's natural to think that negative theology is about using negative words to do theology with. But apophasis isn't about thinking that negative words are always and intrinsically better than positive words – it's obvious they aren't. It's about pointing beyond words to the source. It's about working out how to do God-talk after realizing that, when we ask it to do this work, language fails. As Denys Turner puts it: 'theology means "discourse about God" or "divine discourse", so the expression "apophatic theology" ought to mean something like: "that speech about God which is the failure of speech".'[3]

Apophatic theologians quite often talk about 'negation of negation' for this reason, or 'radical negation': they mean that positive words and negative words both fail God; that 'God is' and 'God is not' both set their sights too low. Both are still stuck in the salami-slicer. Apophasis is the effort of moving away from both positive/affirmative and negative speech about God.

The opposite of apophasis is kataphasis, a movement *towards* speech, deeper into it. Most Christian life is lived kataphatically. There's something intrinsically kataphatic about a faith that begins with God creating a cosmos by speaking, and identifies a particular human life as the pure speech of God translated into flesh and blood (John 1.14). To treasure apophasis is not thereby to devalue kataphasis. But the aim of what follows is to make sense of the idea that we might indeed treasure apophasis, that we might find it exhilarating, life-giving, as powerful as a spiritual emetic, as beautiful as any sacred art; that we might find ourselves moving away from speech into encounter, and thereafter be a little more able to speak of God as God is.

Part 1 will explore some of the biblical roots of apophatic theology. Part 2 sets out some of the classic themes, while Part 3 introduces some of the great pioneers of the apophatic way. In Part 4 we pause to acknowledge some of the allies we might encounter along the way. Part 5 suggests some apophatic practices, in the hope that they will make a living connection, reaching beyond the texts of apophasis (including this one) towards everyday discipleship. Inevitably, this brief selection is very much shaped by my own experience; other guides would point out different sights along the way and offer quite different commentaries. The point, of course, is not the guidebook anyway, but the territory and the beauty and passion of your own journey into it.

Notes

1 From Augustine's sermon 52, *Si comprehendis, non est Deus.*

2 St John of the Cross, *The Ascent of Mount Carmel* 1.13.11, quoting Kieran Kavanaugh's translation in *John of the Cross: Selected Writings* for the Classics of Western Spirituality series (New York: Paulist Press, 1987), p. 79.

3 Denys Turner, *The Darkness of God: Negativity in Christian Mysticism* (Cambridge: Cambridge University Press, 1995), p. 20; italics original.

PART 1

Biblical Roots

Carole Bury, 'Winter Holly', pencil.

Moses:

The Fire and the Cloud

The goal of the spiritual life is to meet God and to keep on meeting God, walking together as friend with friend. Knowing *about* God isn't the goal. The core activity of the spiritual life is prayer; knowing a lot about prayer isn't the same thing as praying.

Rightly, therefore, we prize accounts of what it's like to meet God – at the same time as we recognize that it is our own meeting that matters. The biblical stories of meeting aren't intended as information about historical holy events but as lures, the varied and enticing fly-like decorations fishermen use: they're meant to hook us in, catch us up, draw us into the place of our own meeting. We're supposed to pray these stories, not study them.

For the masters of the apophatic tradition, the two greatest meeting-stories of them all, ones that shine and shimmer with energy, are the meetings of Moses with his God in fire and cloud.

The story of Moses begins in chapter 2 of the book of Exodus. The familiar story of the baby in the bulrushes, who grows up as the adoptive son of Pharaoh's daughter and then flees from Egypt to Midian as a murderer and fugitive from justice, indicates that Moses knew he was a Hebrew but gives no suggestion that he had ever given his people's God more than a passing thought. He is taken completely by surprise, therefore, at the divine initiative, God's decision to catch his attention. This is one of the first key indicators of the apophatic way: it is not a skill we can master, a tradition in which we can become 'expert'. It is a way of exile, powerlessness and vulnerability. William James' study of the classic mystical experience concluded that it had a 'passive' quality – it happens *to* us. Jesus pointed to unprotected street children as examples of the mind that will gain entry to heaven. We can't make God meet us. One word that crops up time and again in descriptions of divine encounter is 'suddenly': it signifies the unexpectedness of God, the absence of any identifiable or manipulatable chain of causes. As the contemporary writer Annie Dillard puts it:

> Although the pearl may be found, it may not be sought. The literature of illumination reveals this above all: although it comes to those who wait for it, it is always, even to the most practised and adept, a gift and a total surprise.[1]

What catches Moses' attention first is fire: a flame, the story says, that burns but does not consume; heat, light – and danger. The presence of God is bright, warm and literally attractive – it draws us towards it. It is threatening – this is not a comfortable spirituality. If we approach God carrying anything that is flammable, we'd better look out! And yet nothing touched by the fire is destroyed by it. The God we meet is creator and transformer, not destroyer.

God's next initiative is to call Moses by his name. We all know what it's like to attend a meeting in which we are not personally involved: we might meet with our child's teacher, for example, attending simply as 'the parent'. The teacher has no interest in our personal history, our interests and goals, only in how we will support our child's learning. Or we might attend a workplace meeting, not in our own right but as a representative of a certain department, or to ensure that a particular skill set is brought to bear on a problem. Meeting God is never like this: it is always personal. God isn't especially interested in the roles we play, rather in the beating heart beneath the costume. But there's more: God already knows Moses' name, and what he is capable of doing. Theologically, you might say, of course that makes sense – the all-knowing creator would know that! But this isn't mere theology, it's a description of what encounter is like. One of the extraordinary things we find is that on the apophatic way we become less and less sure of who we really are: the things that identify us in the world tend to loosen up as we become aware of all the other possibilities within us, all the untold stories about us, all the different perspectives people take on us.

Increasingly unsure of our true nature, we stumble into the presence of a God who knows us better than we know ourselves. We find our true selves, the accounts of meeting tell us, at the moment when we are found by God.

Moses, having been called by name and commissioned to 'bring my people, the children of Israel, out of Egypt' (Exodus 3.10), asks to know the name of God. The name that is disclosed, *'ehyeh 'asher 'ehyeh* (abbreviated in the following verse to the more familiar *Yahweh*, from the third-person form of *'ehyeh*), is gloriously apophatic. A name identifies its bearer, marks them out and distinguishes them from others. It gives to others a degree of power – we can report someone whose name we know to the authorities, we can summon them, bless or curse them, spread true or false information about them and so change the way others approach them. All of this is much harder to do without some kind of name. By naming God we start to 'get a handle' on the divine, we begin to be able to weigh the divine down with all sorts of talk, all sorts of projections – omnipotent, omniscient, omnibenevolent; unresting, unchanging; on our side, smiter of our enemies . . . Yet *'ehyeh 'asher 'ehyeh* isn't quite a name. It's a-name-that-is-no-name. Often translated 'I am who I am', it might also mean 'I cause to be' or 'I will be what I will be'. 'Unnameable', we might paraphrase it, or 'Beyond Naming'.[2] The creation story of Genesis 2 (19—20) suggests that the names of all things derive from Adam: they are human constructions. God is not a being in the same kind of way at all, has no edges or contingent characteristics; God is the divine source, and so can be addressed, invoked, worshipped but not quite named. The Jews, in holy fear, would never *say* the name but use signs instead to refer to it: the unpronounced tetragrammaton, YHWH, or in modern English, 'G-d'.[3]

There is one more telling detail in this story of Moses' first meeting with God: the command to 'take your sandals off your feet, for the place on which you are standing is holy ground' (Exodus 3.5). Most of us have some memory of slipping off our shoes to run across grass, sand or shingle. We know both the delight and the pain of it. The soft skin of our feet is liable to burn on hot sand, be cut by sharp stones, squelch into mud and insects and animal mess we might not even notice with our shoes on. We know, therefore, that walking without shoes makes us notice our vulnerability and pay attention. We also associate barefoot walking with children and with the intimacy of lovers. All of this bears significance for the divine encounter.

It is a fair guess that the shoes Moses had to stoop and take off were made of animal hide – of a rough leather. In other words, they were some other animal's skin. God insists that Moses take them off in order to enter holy ground in his own skin. How often do we try to come to God covered in someone else's skin! How often do we hear people 'leading the intercessions' in church services by reading aloud prayers from books, and if we gently ask them why they didn't write their own prayers, sometimes it'll be for lack of time or some other perfectly good reason, but often they'll look away and say they didn't think their own words were good enough for 'proper prayers'. How astonished would we be if we met up with family members who all insisted on talking to us by reading out things other people had written! Yet we are nervous about speaking with God, and we cover up our weakness with other people's words. It isn't just about prayer either: we tend to put on layer after layer of other people's theology too – ideas about God drawn from books, sermons or conversations; and if we've been on the spiritual journey for a while, we also wear layer after layer of memories and trophies from the scuffles and glories of the past. When at last we find ourselves on the outskirts of holy ground we are muffled up like cartoon Eskimos, and God is going to have to poke us very hard in the ribs if we are going to notice anything at all. There's nothing wrong with all these layers, incidentally, if we're going for a walk on a cold day. But they're going to have to come off if we are to stand in the presence of the living flame.

The encounter with God in the fire is the beginning of Moses' spiritual journey. It is much later – after the plagues, the flight and the Red Sea crossing, when Moses is the acknowledged leader of the pilgrim people of Israel – that he encounters God in the cloud. The story is contained in chapters 19 and 20 of Exodus, where it sets the scene for one of the most significant episodes in the Bible: the giving of the Ten Commandments on Mount Sinai. The meeting between God and Moses is described as taking place in 'thick cloud' (19.9), 'smoke' (19.18) and 'thick darkness' (20.21). It is out of this darkness that the revelation comes – a revelation not about God but about ourselves, how we should live.

Intuitively, we use the language of light to describe both the gradual progress of the spiritual life and the experience of holy encounter itself. We noted that one of the characteristics of fire is its brightness. Jesus is described in John's Gospel as the light of the world, the uncreated light, and in the Nicene Creed as 'light from light'. Paul's dramatic experience of conversion was accompanied by a blinding light. The language of enlightenment, nowadays often associated with Eastern religions, was also used by the early Christian communities to refer to the inner experience of baptism.

The apophatic tradition, however, notices that fire creates smoke and also that too strong a light overpowers our eyes and blinds us as effectively as darkness. In the words of Walter Chalmers Smith's popular hymn:

Immortal, invisible, God only wise,
in light inaccessible hid from our eyes . . .
. . . O help us to see
'tis only the splendour of light hideth thee.

The apophatic tradition notices that the kind of vulnerability we express when we walk barefoot is also experienced when we find ourselves in darkness. Instead of striding confidently ahead, sure of our footing, we find ourselves groping and stumbling. Instead of seeing and knowing ahead of time where we are going, we have to find our way step by step. And it recalls our experience of intimacy, how often we close our eyes to receive a kiss from our beloved, how often we choose warm darkness to explore love, expressing and receiving it in direct contact, skin to skin.

Moses deliberately ascends the mountain, at God's invitation. He separates himself from human company, just as he earlier took off another's skin before the burning bush. He goes to the place where he cannot see, into deep darkness, where none of his existing experience will help, where there is no mental map to guide him. This is the apophatic journey: to have and to use all the knowledge at our disposal, up to the point at which we must go beyond it in search of encounter; to set aside, for the time being at least, everything that helps us when we're in the light – it will only weigh us down in the darkness. What we experience here is that by putting down everything we thought we already knew about God, we don't thereby lessen God in any way but only ourselves. We must become as vulnerable as a child, as unequipped as a beginner, as naked as a lover.

This *via negativa* has often been criticized as a kind of unproductive indulgence. Partly this comes from the themes of separation and darkness. It seems as if the apophatic disciple parts company with most of the people of God, embarks on a solitary journey where everything that might be useful has to be given up, and ends up in a place where nothing can be seen and about which nothing can be said. But the stories of Moses' meetings with God in the fire and the cloud put these experiences in their proper perspective: it is because of these encounters that Moses is able to lead his people to freedom and help them begin to frame a just society. A true encounter with the divine will *always* send us back to the world better equipped to serve it.

The stories of Moses in the fire and the cloud are foundational teachings of apophatic spirituality. They speak to us of the suddenness of holy encounter, the way it seems simply to happen to us, at God's initiative; of the way God's presence entices and burns, but without destroying; of the intimately personal nature of these meetings, where we find that God knows us better than we know ourselves; of the absolute requirement to come to God in our own skin, not protected by someone else's; of the beyondness of this God, beyond our naming and beyond our sight; and of the imperative, after the meeting has ended, to return to God's people and make ourselves useful. Exodus (13.21–2) tells us that throughout their time of wandering in the wilderness, Moses' people were guarded and guided by the fire and the cloud.

Notes

1 Annie Dillard, *Pilgrim at Tinker Creek* (New York: HarperCollins, 1998), p. 35.

2 Richard Kearney, in *The God Who May Be: A Hermeneutics of Religion* (Bloomington, IN: University of Indiana Press, 2001), p. 26, discussing Exodus 3.15, 'This is my name for ever . . .', notes 'The word for "forever" in this verse is spelled in such a way that it takes the form of a word which normally says to "hide the Name."'

3 The sacred name was not always unpronounceable among the Jews, but the practice seems to have taken hold from the sixth century before Christ onwards – see Diarmaid MacCulloch, *Silence: A Christian History* (London: Penguin, 2014), p. 26.

The Song of Songs

The presence in the midst of the Hebrew Bible of a book of unabashed erotic poetry, which doesn't mention God at all, is a bracing challenge to anyone who looks to the Jewish or Christian traditions for a tidy theology and a safe God. Unsurprisingly, then, the Song of Songs tends to be neglected as far as popular understanding of the faith is concerned; many Christians are largely or entirely ignorant of the book, having never heard it read or preached on in church, unless perhaps they have heard this beautiful passage as a wedding reading, or in one of its musical settings:

> Set me as a seal upon your heart,
>   as a seal upon your arm;
> for love is strong as death,
>   jealousy is fierce as the grave.
> Its flashes are flashes of fire,
>   the very flame of the LORD.
> Many waters cannot quench love,
>   neither can floods drown it.
> If a man offered for love
>   all the wealth of his house,
>   he would be utterly despised. (8.6–7)

In the Christian mystical tradition, on the other hand, the reverse is true: the Song of Songs is a foundational text, one of the core biblical anchors of apophatic spirituality. Like an exceptional single malt whisky, it contains the characteristic flavours of apophasis in a powerfully concentrated and richly complex, heady and intoxicating form.

The Song of Songs is remarkable, first of all, for its full-blooded sensuality. To use an old-fashioned word, it is thoroughly 'carnal' – meaning fleshly, embodied. It is not merely erotic: the poetry celebrates embodied existence not only in the act of love but in the appreciation of the beauty of the body (1.5: 'I am very dark, but lovely') and the glory of physical energy (2.8–9 'Behold, he comes, leaping over the mountains, bounding over the hills. My beloved is like a gazelle or a young stag'). All the senses are celebrated – the sight of the beloved's beauty, the sound of his voice, the scent of anointed and perfumed skin, the taste of shared fruit, the touch of an adored hand. For the Song, the full range of human experience carries spiritual meaning: there is nothing that is 'beneath' God – all is included.

In those Christian cultures that have succumbed to a dualistic view, where soul is spiritual and good and body is gross and bad, the Song's celebration of sensuality, if read literally, would be frankly embarrassing. However, we shouldn't overstate this problem. It seemed obvious to most commentators that these texts are to be taken allegorically. The God who is never explicitly named in the text is present everywhere in it – in desire, in beauty, in energy and of course in love. The Jewish prophets had made marriage one of their most frequent images for the relationship between God and the chosen people; later Christian commentators read the text as speaking not merely of the relation between God and the Church – or, more accurately, Christ and his Bride – but between God and the individual soul. Reading the poems in this context, they speak powerfully of the mutual delight of God and humanity, and of both human desire for God's presence and our sense of desolation when we fail to encounter him. And since God does not actually have a material body, all the sensual imagery is metaphorical – it is pointing to the truth that we encounter the divine beyond the mind, in a way of knowing that is as far superior to the mind as the mind is superior to the body.

But there comes a point where a completely spiritualized reading of the Song just trips up on the sheer exuberance of the poems' sensuality: if we are supposed to be mentally subtracting the physical detail from the text as we hear or read it, why does it revel so much precisely in this detail?

Your hair is like a flock of goats,
  leaping down the slopes of Gilead.
Your teeth are like a flock of shorn ewes
  that have come up from the washing,
all of which bear twins,
  and not one among them has lost its young.
Your lips are like a scarlet thread,
  and your mouth is lovely.
Your cheeks are like halves of a pomegranate
  behind your veil. (4.1–3)

This question brings us to the point where a mystical or contemplative reading of the Song becomes fully apophatic: it isn't just that the sensual language needs to be understood spiritually, rather that the sensuality of the language carries significance in its own right, significance that has to be fully affirmed as well as denied. (Many of the medieval mystics worked through the implications of this language – hence, for example, the legends of mystical marriage among saints such as Catherine of Siena.) Sensual knowledge, unlike abstract theoretical knowledge, involves the embodied participation of the knower – the knower has to give of him- or herself, and is as much (if not more) the object as the subject of the knowing. Put in those words, this sounds like abstract philosophy, but it is really common sense: we all know from experience that we will never truly know the ones we love unless we make ourselves vulnerable to them, give ourselves away to them. Only then will we see the depths of their character – but our own is disclosed at the same time, often to our shame!

Sensual knowing – like the famous parable of the blind men and the elephant – is also inescapably partial and particular: we know only what 'it' looks like from this particular angle, what it smells like in this instant, what it feels like in *our* hands. There are only two ways we can know what it's like from other standpoints: either go there ourselves or listen very carefully while others tell us. Always, always there is the possibility of an as yet unexplored perspective that will revolutionize our understanding, or a paradigm shift in whose heat all our earlier interpretations will fry to a crisp. Always, always we need to carry our beautiful encounters as the lightest and most disposable of baggage, lest the experiences of the past become obstacles to future meetings.

For all the lovers' delight in the sight and sound of one another in the Song, there is a strong direction in the poems, an urge to touch and taste. The senses are not, in the end, equal: vision and sound reveal things that are at a distance from us, but scent has to be closer, touch more so, and of course taste closest of all. Whereas some kinds of knowledge can be gained merely by study, wisdom cannot be separated from embodied encounter: the Latin word for 'wisdom', *sapientia* (from which we derive the ironic-sounding *homo sapiens*), shares a common root with *sapor*, 'flavour'. Wisdom is a knowledge that savours, then: it comes via palate, olfactory nerve and fingertips. So if these poems tell us anything of the relationship between God and the soul (or Church), they seem to be pointing us away from the kind of knowledge you get from standing back and observing, and towards the kind you get through intimacy, through touch and taste.

Like the divine flame in the bush that burns but is never consumed, so the words of the Song show the lovers savouring one another without ever exhausting beauty and delight. Words are piled giddily on one another. A. S. Byatt comments:

> There is an element of excess, of too much, too much fruit; too many riches, too much landscape, too much architecture, eyes like fishpools, nose like a tower of Lebanon, breasts like twin roes, a creature who in one verse is fair as the moon, clear as the sun, and terrible as an army with banners. When the navel is compared to a round goblet, which wanteth not liquor and the belly is immediately afterwards compared to a heap of wheat set about with lilies, the effect is to make the wine and wheat richly present and the human body shadowy, vanishing, mysterious.[1]

This exuberance is another characteristic of the apophatic spirituality: all words add something to our understanding of God, all images are affirmed as well as denied. No words exhaust this truth. The overabundance of words and images paradoxically undoes itself, as Byatt says: far from eliminating mystery, the folding together of different and even contradictory images creates a conceptual space marked by mystery – this is 'verbal magic'.[2]

In our highly sexualized culture, the use of sexual imagery to signify spiritual encounter makes sense on a fairly intuitive level. We understand what it has to say about intimacy, about knowledge that comes through exploratory delight, about appetite that even when satisfied is not exhausted but grows greater. We understand too how in this kind of encounter we are joined with what we love, and find ourselves more fully even as we lose the ability to distinguish clearly between what belongs to the self and what belongs to the beloved.

We might have to stretch a little further, though, to appreciate the Song's emphasis on eating. In fact nothing can be more intimate, nothing a closer symbol of union, than eating. What we eat and drink passes into our inmost being, is absorbed into our blood and energy, is transformed into the very stuff of our bodies. We are totally dependent on what we consume – light, air, liquids, solids. The thirteenth-century Flemish mystic Hadewijch says: 'Love's most intimate union is through eating, tasting, and seeing interiorly'.[3] The Song's emphasis on love's banqueting house (2.4) is surely one of the roots of Jesus' own practice of table-fellowship and of the Christian Eucharist.

Desire, union, delight, intimate knowledge: these are the primary apophatic themes of the Song of Songs. Almost equally important, however, are the secondary themes of darkness, loss and yearning quest:

> On my bed by night
> I sought him whom my soul loves;
>   I sought him, but found him not . . .
> My beloved put his hand to the latch,
>   and my heart was thrilled within me.
> I arose to open to my beloved,
>   and my hands dripped with myrrh,

my fingers with liquid myrrh,
   on the handles of the bolt.
I opened to my beloved,
   but my beloved had turned and gone.
My soul failed me when he spoke.
I sought him, but found him not;
   I called him, but he gave no answer. (3.1–2; 5.4–6)

These haunting verses have often been read as a description of the experience the mystics call the 'dark night of the soul': a time of desolation, when the soul that has had some beautiful encounter with God finds itself alone again, unable to find its way back to the presence. Whereas atop Sinai was a darkness of presence, where Moses' blindness opened his heart to holy encounter, the Song's darkness has moments of sweet presence interspersed with times of ghastly, groaning absence. Such 'dark nights', in a precise sense, refer to very particular stages of growth into spiritual maturity, but a more mundane version of the experience is surely known by every-one who prays. The third-century teacher Origen confessed:

> Then she [the Bride in the Song of Songs] looks longingly for the Bridegroom who has shown himself and then disappeared. This happens often throughout the Song of Songs and can be under-stood by anyone who has experienced it himself. Often, as God is my witness, I have felt that the Bridegroom was drawing near to me and was as close to me as possible. Then all of a sudden he has gone away and I have not been able to find the object of my search.[4]

The Song describes with absolute poetic accuracy what it feels like to have been touched by God and then find the moment past, or to have felt so close to encounter but been disappointed. Importantly, it sets such moments in the wider context of a generous and mutual loving delight. As a foundational text of the apophatic tradition, this aspect of the Song has two further things to teach us. First, that there is no final encounter. Unlike the fairy stories in which a marriage ensures that the lovers will live 'happily ever after', in the journey towards union with God, divine encounter comes with

15

no guarantee of stability or permanence. This may be true to our experience but it is nonetheless a shocking reversal of the prophets' theme, which always contrasts divine faithfulness with human faithlessness. For the prophets, God never 'goes away' – it is Israel that wanders. Here in the Song the irony is that it is precisely the lover's delight, and her preparation, that make her 'lose' the beloved. She hears his hand on the latch and is so overwhelmed by her heart's answering leap that she is too slow to welcome him in. She has been so busy making herself beautiful in anticipation of his arrival that her ointment-slicked hands slip clumsily on the bolt and again she is just too slow – the beloved, clearly, is not one for hanging around. Once again these poems speak truth with breathtaking accuracy. How often must we confess that it is our anticipation, our preparation and our delight that make us lose the moment; how often it is our fantasy or memory of divine encounter that makes the gift of the present slip through our hands.

Second, the Song suggests that the loving soul has more to lose on her journey than the hoped-for encounter – more that she *must* lose, somehow, if she is to find the beloved once more. In the second poem (5.2–8) on this theme, as in the first, the yearning lover wanders the city, looking for the beloved, and as she wanders she encounters the watchmen. Only in the second poem, however, do the watchmen seem hostile: 'they beat me, they wounded me, they took away my mantle (5.7 RSV). The 'mantle' – cloak, outer covering – reminds us of Moses' sandals, that covering which is *not our own skin*, not the pure authenticity of our own selves, the place where we can truly encounter the holy. The implication seems to be that the lover is naked under her cloak – only a couple of verses earlier we are told that she has put off her garment. Gregory of Nyssa, identifying the mantle with the garment, noted shrewdly that the mantle seems to have appeared again as soon as she took it off – as if, however hard we try to rid ourselves of the layers that insulate us against the divine current, they reappear as fast as we can peel them off.[5]

Weaving these last insights back together, we find the Song suggesting to us that a very great deal of our religious activity, our spiritual lives, is spent ornamenting and beautifying precisely the stuff that in the end we'll need to get rid of, the stuff that becomes an obstacle and a barrier to our authentic encounter with God. Some of it we may be able to strip off for ourselves. The rest will be more painful.

Notes

1 A. S. Byatt, 'The Song of Solomon', in *Revelations: Personal Responses to the Books of the Bible* (Edinburgh: Canongate, 2006), p. 167.

2 'Verbal magic' is Francis Landy's verdict in *The Literary Guide to the Bible*, ed. Robert Alter and Frank Kermode (London: Collins, 1987), p. 307.

3 Hadewijch of Antwerp, *Poems in Couplets* 16, 'Love's Seven Names', ll. 37–8, in the translation by Mother Columba Hart for the Classics of Western Spirituality series (New York: Paulist Press, 1980), p. 353.

4 Origen, *Sermons on the Song of Songs* 1,7, as cited in Olivier Clément, *The Roots of Christian Mysticism* (London: New City, 1993), p. 189.

5 Gregory of Nyssa's *Commentary on the Song*, in Migne's *Patrologia Graeca*, 1029A f.

John the Baptist, Apophatic Prophet

John the Baptist figures in all the biblical Gospels, but only in the Fourth Gospel's characteristically distinctive depiction is the Baptist an apophatic prophet. Here John is the first to model for us what it means to live a life centred on Christ rather than self; to proclaim a gospel message while knowing in our bones that we do not fully understand it ourselves; to find our own identities thrown into question while we live out the more fundamental question: Who is Jesus? Is he the one for whom our hearts yearn or simply the projection of those yearnings? If he does not fulfil all our hopes, does that mean he is not The One, or simply that his truth is deeper than our poor hopes? The Baptist, more than any other biblical figure, shows us how to be faithful witnesses and disciples, not *in spite of* our own ignorance and inauthenticity but by recognizing and working *with and through* them.

John the Gospel-writer brings his characters into focus as carefully as a dramatist brings characters onstage: their first and last words are especially significant. Notice, then, the first things the Baptist says in the Fourth Gospel: he is answering questions from Jewish priests and Levites about his identity:

> He confessed . . . 'I am not the Christ.'
> And they asked him, 'What then? Are you Elijah?'
> He said, 'I am not.'
> 'Are you the prophet?'
> And he answered, 'No.' (1.20–21)

To see the pattern even more starkly, focus just on John's words:

'I am not the Christ.'
'I am not.'
'No.'
'I am not the Christ'; 'I am not'; 'No.'

John's first prophetic utterance is quickly honed down, like a modern-day advertising slogan or a Zen *koan*, to this one word, 'No' or 'not' – 'Just no! I'm not anything you can nail down with a definition. I'm not a repeat of something you already know about. I'm not here to pander to your domesticated religion.' The message fizzes with significance, partly because of the contrast with Jesus. Remember Paul, in his second letter to the Corinthians, saying that with Jesus 'it is always Yes' (1.19). Remember the significance of Jesus' 'I am' sayings, the distinctive 'I am' of this Fourth Gospel – 'I am the bread of life' (6.35), 'I am the true vine' (15.1) and so on. Most of all, remember that 'I am who I am' is the no-name of God (Exodus 3.14), a name so holy that in righteous fear it could not be spoken among the Jews.

The question 'Who is this?' sounds like a key signature throughout all the Gospels, but especially the fourth. The question is posed and provoked by Jesus himself: 'Who do people say that I am? Who do you say that I am?' (Matthew 16.13–14; Mark 8.27–29; Luke 9.18–20); in John's Gospel its characteristic form is 'Whom do you seek?' (John 18.4; 20.15; and compare 1.38). John the Baptist's 'I am not', which opens the earthly section of the Gospel's account of Jesus' life and work, finds its counterpoint in the great revelation scene in Gethsemane, where Jesus declares 'I am', two words like a lion's roar three times in three verses. Jesus' words can be superficially heard as a mundane declaration to the guards – 'I am the man you have been sent to arrest' – but they resonate much more deeply. Jesus declares that he is the one whom everyone is seeking, the one for whom all human hearts yearn. And he takes upon himself the very name, the name-that-is-no-name, of God.

Where Jesus' message is 'Yes, I am', John's is 'No, I am not'. When he does respond positively to the demand that he identify himself,

John offers a relational identity. His identity is not self-contained, self-referencing, self-fulfilling; who he is is only clear in relation to Jesus and to the other prophets of the Hebrew tradition. As 'a voice crying in the wilderness', John speaks the words of others (John 1.23; Isaiah 40.3), and speaks about one who is beyond him.

In the other three Gospels, John's message is about sin and repentance. Here in the Fourth Gospel it is a subtler and more radical message of negation, a message not simply proclaimed but lived – the Baptist is presented as one who 'walks the talk'. The path of the Messiah is prepared by what Jesus will elsewhere call 'denying oneself' (Matthew 16.24; Mark 8.34; Luke 9.23), by recognizing how far we fall short of living our own lives, how utterly insubstantial and thoroughly dependent we are, for good and for ill, on human others and on forces beyond ourselves, and finally on God, the source of life itself.

John and Jesus together show us humanity in itself and humanity indwelt by God. Jesus' 'I am' and John's 'I am not' are not simply statements about a particular identity – that Jesus is the Messiah and John is not. They are statements about our experience of living: that only God simply 'is', while humanity comes into being in relationship to God and to others, finds itself constantly struggling to become what it can be, co-creates itself in partnership with others, is always living and dying together. Nor is the Baptist's 'I am not' an admission of failure. It is a mark of mental and spiritual health because it is in and through the 'I am not' that the Baptist fulfils his own vocation: to prepare the way for the Lord's anointed.

John the Baptist's great declaration of 'I am not' is made on the first particular day of the Fourth Gospel's account. On the next day, a second and a third theme emerge. 'I myself did not know him', John says twice (1.31, 33). Here the existential (being) negation of 'I am not' is matched by an epistemological (knowing) negation, 'I knew not'. Whereas John's 'I am not' might perhaps be heard as a development of the characteristic modesty of the Hebrew prophets – think of Isaiah's 'I am a man of unclean lips' and Jeremiah's 'I am only a youth' (Isaiah 6.5; Jeremiah 1.6, and compare Moses' 'Who am I that I should go?' (Exodus 3.11)) – his 'I knew not' sets him further apart from his predecessors. The Hebrew Scriptures tell stories of God's true prophets struggling to distinguish themselves from false prophets (see for example the story of Micaiah in 1 Kings 22, and Jeremiah ch. 28); the true prophets such as Isaiah declare 'the word of the Lord' with utter confidence (see for example Isaiah 42.5; 43.1; 45.1); and the book of Deuteronomy includes instructions for distinguishing between true and false prophets (18.15–22). By comparison with John the Baptist, the earlier prophets' confidence borders on pugnacity. They know how the future will turn out. They know they are set apart; while relatively powerless and ignorant in themselves, they are confident in receiving from God detailed knowledge of the future, of the will and ways of God. How modest John is by contrast! In the Fourth Gospel, John claims to have only partial sight, only a dim presentiment, only a provisional message.

If the first theme is 'I am not' and the second 'I knew not', the third theme given to John in this Gospel concerns sight, and this is the first fully positive statement by John: 'Behold! . . . I saw . . . I have seen and have borne witness' (1.29–34). Here the Gospel-writer picks up on the themes of his Prologue, themes of light and vision. John the Baptist, as the first person in this account to recognize Jesus, is the role model for all of us. The key, we are shown, is not in being or knowing but in seeing, encountering and recognizing; and in order to do that we need to set aside our fixations on self and status, on what we have achieved, on our past history and our future hope. We need simply to pay attention, to have 'eyes to see' as the beyond comes near.

'I am not'
'I did not know'
'Behold . . . I have seen and have borne witness.'

So far we have noticed how John the Baptist's apophatic denials contrast with the consistent affirmations of Jesus. But there is one other striking contrast. All the Gospels contain the story of Peter's triple denial of Christ on the night of his arrest, before the cock crowed, but only the Fourth Gospel contains two contrasted sets of denials: the Baptist's and Peter's. In John's Gospel, Peter's words are twice 'I am not' (18.17, 25); the third denial is simply reported – 'Peter again denied it' (18.27). Both Peter and the Baptist speak the words that are the opposite of Christ's 'I am'. In that sense, we might say, they both 'deny'. But what Peter is denying is his relationship to Jesus, whereas by denying any claim to independent identity, John is precisely affirming his dependence on Jesus. Thus the Gospel describes John's words as 'testimony' and 'confession' (1.19, 20), but not Peter's; and describes Peter's 'I am not' as a denial but John's 'I am not' as not-denial. John's self-denial is a witness to truth, whereas Peter utters falsehood to save himself. Peter's denial is later undone, in the triple question 'Do you love me?' in this Gospel's last chapter, and its heartfelt response: 'You know I love you.' John's denial, by contrast, is never to be undone: it is the pattern for us to follow.

In this deliberate contrast, unique to the Fourth Gospel, we are shown two different ways of denial. Many people who encounter the apophatic tradition for the first time shy away from it – it seems too close to Peter's denial. They confuse holy denial with loss of faith, and – although they might not use these words – anxious concerns about blasphemy and apostasy often rise up, putting their sense of salvation itself in peril. However, they should be comforted. First, the Baptist shows us how to make this practice serve our encounter with Jesus, not undermine it. He shows us that the true object of the apophatic denial is the self, with its particular baggage of experience, prejudice and projection, and not the One we seek to see. And second, although Peter's denial is horrifying, not least as regards his own understanding of who he is in relation to Jesus, it is a stage on his journey, not a dead end. How could we know whether Peter would ever have come to that later deep declaration of love – not just any old love but perfect *friendship* – if he had not achieved the self-knowledge unlocked by his denial? Hesitantly and with great caution, we may have to admit that – even though it may not be something we are called to take on as a deliberate spiritual practice – sometimes the more painful denial might even be a way forward into deeper relationship for us.

Although John the Baptist continues to be discussed and his ministry compared to Jesus', his own voice is last heard in the Fourth Gospel towards the end of chapter 3, in response to a suggestion that he might see Jesus as a competitor: 'look, he is baptizing, and all are going to him' (3.26). John responds by comparing Jesus to a bridegroom, and himself to a groomsman. He is, he says, 'full of joy' (3.29). In his final words, John underscores the key role he plays in this Gospel. He is the apophatic prophet par excellence, both announcing the provisionality and incompleteness of his own knowledge, and living out the negative way as self-abandonment, self-emptying, in honour of the Word who became flesh and dwelt among us. What fills John with joy is not his own life but Jesus': this is the Fourth Gospel's demonstration of St Paul's insight, 'It is no longer I who live, but Christ who lives in me' (Galatians 2.20). John the Baptist, the last of Jesus' predecessors in the great Hebrew prophetic tradition, is arguably the greatest of them all (see the claim Jesus makes in Matthew 11.11: 'Truly, I say to you, among those born of women there has arisen no one greater than John the Baptist'); and his greatness consists precisely in his understanding that he does not have the full truth, does not have the whole vision, is not competing with Jesus for God's grace or for human followers, but finds his own truest, deepest self most completely when he finds Jesus. The parting words (3.30) of this great and wonderful prophet are a call to apophatic discipleship: 'He must increase, but I must decrease.'

Jesus:

Word and Silence

To the apophatic witness of John's 'No, I am not' we have contrasted Jesus' 'Yes, I am.' The Fourth Gospel begins by identifying the man Jesus of Nazareth as the Word who 'became flesh and dwelt among us' (1.14), that same word by which God created the heavens and the earth and all that is in them. Christ, embodied as a Galilean peasant, is the very Logos of God – a term that contains not just the sense of 'spoken word' but also of 'plan', 'reason', 'principle', 'order', 'thought'. In the person of Jesus, this Gospel intimates, God is doing something world-changing, inaugurating a new epoch. The God who had not spoken directly, friend-to-friend, with humanity since the time of the Patriarchs, whose conversations with Moses were of such dangerous intensity that they had to happen safely away from the mass of the people, and who for generations had communicated more distantly, through the ambiguous and indirect speech of the prophets, this God was now speaking directly, in the same way that he did in the very beginning, yet now addressed to everyone. Jesus, the Alpha and Omega (Revelation 1.8; 21.6; 22.13), God's first word and his last, is 'spoken' into life, a life extraordinary yet common, shared, available, tangible. In Jesus, God's own plan for humanity is made flesh and blood.

Through the medium of written words, the fourth evangelist directs our attention towards spoken words, and through and beyond them to the articulation of divinity in a life lived blazingly beneath the mundane sky. This Gospel is full of apophatic pointers: Jesus, the Way, the Truth and the Life (John 14.6), demonstrates that truth is not words but flesh and bone, not all at once but step by step (not End but Way), not still but pulsing (not Sacrifice but Life). Only this Gospel crowns Jesus' crucifixion with the trium-phant cry 'It is finished!' (19.30); the same Gospel alone tells us that Jesus made clear to his friends that his Truth was *un*finished (14.25–26).

None of the Gospels quite ends, of course; each abandons writing in its own characteristic way. From John the Evangelist we have end without end: multiple stories of resurrection encounter, what looks like an ending in 20.30–31, then succeeded by another chapter concluding in 21.25: 'Now there are also many other things that Jesus did. Were every one of them to be written, I suppose that the world itself could not contain the books that would be written.' That repeated 'written' recalls an earlier comment about writing the identity of Jesus, Pilate's response in 19.22 to those who objected to the cross's superscription, 'The King of the Jews': 'What I have written I have written.' The words inscribed on the cross tell the truth that kills Truth. Perhaps all written words about him will do the same, unless we include this crucial apophatic rider: there is more truth yet than could ever be written.

Unlike the ascetic John, Jesus was known for his enjoyment of life, including his scandalous habits of table fellowship with the despised and the wicked, his insistence on prioritizing life over law and his bordering-on-casual approach to questions of purity. There was clearly a great deal of talking, both formal teaching (through dialogue, in the rabbinic manner) and informal conversation. There is a deeper asceticism in his teaching though, not simply a matter of dietary abstinence, sexual continence or daily frugality, but the denial of self and the way of the cross (Matthew 16.24–25): 'If anyone would come after me, let him deny himself and take up his cross and follow me. For whoever would save his life will lose it, but whoever loses his life for my sake will find it.'

To our familiar eyes it is easy to miss just how much of Jesus' life and teaching, and the good news as told by the early Church, was a performance of a grand and consistent denial or negation. It starts at the beginning of Mark's Gospel proclamation: 'The beginning of the gospel (*euangelion*) of Jesus Christ, the Son of God.' Rowan Williams explains:

An *euangelion* was a press release from the Buckingham Palace or Downing Street of the day announcing a significant event of public interest: the emperor's son had got engaged or had been invested with some dignity, a princess had had a baby, the army had defeated the Germans, a city on the border of the Persian Empire had been captured . . . [it] is a message about something that alters the climate in which people live, changing the politics and the possibilities; it transforms the landscape of social life.[1]

The *euangelion* of Jesus Christ is a proclamation of regime change. It announces the beginning of the reign of God. The power of every Caesar and all their puppet regimes is denied: 'for the kingdom and the power and the glory are yours, for ever and ever'.

Having begun with this great contradiction of the world's authorities, the good-news story continues in the narrative of Jesus' life. His teachings consistently contradict expectations. His followers are commended to follow the examples of an unjust steward (Luke 16.1–9), of a despised outsider (Luke 10.29–37), of a soldier of the occupation (Luke 7.9). He tells stories in which Yahweh appears as a ridiculous figure – a master who waits on his own servants (Luke 12.37), a doting father who is oblivious to his own honour (Luke 15.11–32), an absentee landlord whose failure to understand his tenants' desperation gets his own heir killed (Luke 20.9–19). He raises Messianic expectations, only to subvert them – most clearly in the dramatic curtain-raiser to his public ministry, as narrated by Luke (4.16–31): Jesus appears in the synagogue in his home town, and reads from one of the most treasured Messianic prophecies, Isaiah 61. He claims for himself Isaiah's calling 'to proclaim good news to the poor . . . liberty to the captives and recovering of sight to the blind, to set at liberty those who are oppressed, to proclaim the year of the Lord's favour', and yet he leaves out the best bit (to his audience) of all, 'the day of vengeance of our God' (Isaiah 61.2), and the following verses, which speak of the restoration of Israel and their imperial subjugation of foreign nations. Kenneth Bailey analyses this passage at length, commenting:

Here in Isaiah the anticipated golden age of the Messiah promised great things. With the coming of the anointed one of God, all the hard work would be done by foreigners, and they, the settlers, would become wealthy, thanks to the labor of others . . . Jesus, the local boy, came to town as an itinerant rabbi and was given a chance to have his say. His audience of settlers understood the text of Isaiah 61 along the lines just indicated. With everyone listening intently, Jesus chose this familiar and deeply beloved passage, but to their shock and amazement he stopped reading at the very point at which judgment and servitude is pronounced on the Gentiles . . . He announced the dawning of the messianic age as an event that was taking place in him before their eyes . . . They must have been thinking something along the lines of:

'What is the matter with this boy? He has quoted one of our favorite texts, but has omitted some of its most important verses. In the process he has turned a text of judgment into a text of mercy. This is outrageous!'[2]

This Jesus consistently overturns things, both in word ('So the last will be first, and the first last'; Matthew 20.16) and in deed (the moneychangers' tables in the Temple; John 2.13–22).

It isn't just what he says and does but even who he is. Norms of social worth are contradicted by the incarnation of God as a callous-fingered artisan. The place of the glory of the presence of God is no longer the Temple but a beating heart within a too vulnerable cage of ribs. The Chosen One is the servant of all. The one who surrenders himself to the forces of injustice is the champion who wins the cosmic battle. A pierced and broken body is the seed from which all life shoots.

St Paul saw what it amounted to: revolution, the turning of everything around. He cannot express it without paradox: the wisdom of God is made manifest in folly (1 Corinthians 1.25); we live by sharing in Christ's death (Romans 6.4). Appearances must be denied, their opposites affirmed. As Tom Wright points out, Paul's description of the work of the cross (Colossians 2.13–15):

is of course deliberately ironic. What seemed to be happening as Jesus of Nazareth hung in agony on the cross was that the 'rulers and authorities' were celebrating their triumph over *him*, having stripped him of his clothes and held him up to public contempt. No, insists Paul, once you learn the meaning of the gospel, you have to see everything inside out.[3]

Diarmaid MacCulloch speaks of a 'silence at the heart of Christian literature' – an apophatic 'vanishing point' in the middle of the kataphatic account of God's dealings with his people: 'The New Testament is thus a literature with a blank at its centre, whereof it cannot speak; yet this blank is also its obsessive focus.'[4] This silence concerns Jesus' resurrection. As MacCulloch points out, although we have descriptions of what happened before and after, there is no biblical account of the resurrection itself, either as event or as state of being. Scripture does not follow Jesus into the tomb, nor venture further into his post-resurrection life than the external appearance and activities. In this absence of words, as in the absence of the dead body, space is blown open; energy, matter and spirit are transfigured.

Even in the accounts of resurrection appearances there are 'apophatic markers' if we care to trace them. There is the logical inconsistency of John's account of a Risen Lord sufficiently immaterial to shimmy through a locked door (20.26) but still possessed of a digestive tract (21.9–14; also Luke 24.30). There is the testimony of both Luke and John to the disciples' astounding capacity for *not recognizing* the one who has been so dear, and John's implicit suggestion that the risen Jesus encounters us not as he is but as we are able to receive him – as a gardener to one who comes to a garden to meet him (20.11–18), to fishermen at a lakeside over a fish breakfast (21.4–13), as inquisitor, comforter and judge to one consumed with guilt (21.15–19), as unmoving presence to the one 'who had been reclining at table close to him' (21.20). Most powerfully, there is Mark's account of the appearance of the risen Christ, an account not contained within the text at all but in the hearts of those who are called (16.6–7): 'he is not here . . . he is going before you . . . you will see him.'

The silence does not begin at Gethsemane, though: it has been a constant and growing theme in the Gospels. There is the silence of what is not told, concerning Jesus' early years for example. There are the silences of his choosing: the times of retreat in the wilderness and to other quiet spaces. There is his interior silence: the stillness dramatized in the stories of the calming of storms (Matthew 8.23–27; 14.22–33), the peace that blazes out in the glory of the Transfiguration (Matthew 17.1–8), and his instruction to others to find that still centre as their 'inner room', the ground from which to approach God (Matthew 6.6). Later there is what MacCulloch calls 'one of the most eloquent quiet stares in human history', the silent gaze of Jesus as Peter denies him (Luke 22.61).[5]

In the shortest and probably the earliest of the Gospels, silence is laid like a muzzle on the lips of those who would proclaim Jesus the Messiah: 'See that you say nothing to anyone' (Mark 1.44); 'And he strictly charged them to tell no one about him' (Mark 8.30). What could they have said, what kind of Messiah could they have made him out to be, before they had seen the shape of his identity disclosed on the cross? At Calvary, at last, the truth is proclaimed – though even now, ambiguously – from the place least expected, from the mouth of a Roman centurion: 'Truly this man was the Son of God' (Mark 15.39). Thereafter the injunction is reversed; *now* it is 'go, tell' (Mark 16.7) – although his followers signally fail in the telling: 'they said nothing to anyone, for they were afraid' (16.8).

A little story about Jesus' transformative use of silence has made its way into the Fourth Gospel (8.3–11).[6] The Pharisees set Jesus a trap, where every possible option is calculated to defeat him. The question of what to do with the nameless 'woman taken in adultery' is nothing to do with her, with her personal situation, the circumstances of the case: she is just the means to a greater end. If Jesus is consistent in his teaching of forgiveness, he will explicitly and publicly contradict the law of Moses. If he upholds that law and demands that she be stoned, he will contradict himself. If he admits uncertainty or confusion, his authority will buckle.

Jesus' response contains three elements, wrapped in a fourth: silence. He scribbles in the dust; he engages the personal histories of his audience; he speaks words of compassion and challenge to the woman. By means of silence Jesus creates a space in which expectations are shifted, the hidden is uncovered and the freedom to act differently – to be *converted* – emerges within hearts and minds.

By bending and scribbling, he draws attention away from abstract questions, to the particularities and bodies involved – this body, his; and that body, hers – in this place; to the soft evanescence of the dust that will claim all bodies, and the hard stones that can break them; to the fleeting nature of life; and to the pity of God (Psalm 103.13–14 RSV):

> As a father pities his children,
>   so the LORD pities those who fear him.
> For he knows our frame;
>   he remembers that we are dust.

In the face of the world's cruel contradictions, Jesus enacts the creative power of apophatic silence. Out of it come words to spring the trap.

In all the Gospels, silence thickens and congeals at the point where Jesus is put on trial. Jesus' way of self-emptying (Philippians 2.7) brings him to give himself – his body and his life – up to men of power. He steps out of action into passivity, out of speech into increasing silence. In the Gospel scenes of trial and execution, 'like a sheep that before its shearers is silent' (Isaiah 53.7) he is the still centre around which the words and actions of others disclose their true natures.

Here, as in the encounter with the woman taken in adultery, none of the world's words are adequate to the truth. Jesus is silent before his accusers not out of wilfulness but simply because he has nothing to say that they would be able to hear. His silence is God's refusal to make conversation in a world where love is bound and truth is beaten. In Matthew's (27.11) and Luke's (23.3) accounts of his trials, Pilate asks Christ directly, 'Are you the King of the Jews?'; the answer returned is 'You say so.' Like an ebbing tide, speech is withdrawing now, ceding ground to more brutal encounter: the words spoken belong to the world, with its hierarchies of power and its obsession with rulers. In the presence of the mute Word of Life, the true nature of such speech is unmasked: these are words intent on judgement and death. In the Fourth Gospel, Jesus' trial before the High Priest demonstrates the failure of worldly speech to make any spark of living contact with God's Word. A set-piece dialogue between Christ and Pilate presses the point home – Pilate has no words to speak of him as he is (John 18.33–38):

'Are you the King of the Jews?'
  'Do you say this of your own accord, or did others say it to you about me?'
'Am I a Jew? Your own nation and the chief priests have delivered you over to me. What have you done?'
  'My kingdom is not of this world. If my kingdom were of this world, my servants would have been fighting, that I might not be delivered over . . . But my kingdom is not from the world.'
'So you are a king?'
  'You say that I am a king. For this purpose I was born, and for this purpose I have come into the world, to bear witness to the truth. Everyone who is of the truth listens to my voice.'
'What is truth?'

Pilate, the pantomime fool, does not wait for a response to his question, while everyone in the Gospel's audience knows the unvoiced answer, which has sounded throughout this Gospel – *I AM!*

The Gospels were written for church communities that celebrated all Jesus meant by gathering around broken bread and wine outpoured. Small wonder, then, that when texts emerged to communicate his life and work, they too fractured words and spilt meaning. They tell us of what cannot be told. They point to a life that contradicted all the world's signifying. These rich apophatic texts demonstrate what happens when divine words break back into human speech.

By cruel coincidence, the first atomic bomb detonated in war, over Hiroshima in 1945, was dropped on the day the Church celebrates the Feast of the Transfiguration. The 6th of August marks in our calendars the hellish opposition between the deadly brightness of human power and the shining glory of divine presence. It is the same contrast, made visible in space and time, as that between human speech and divine in the Gospel accounts of Jesus' trials. R. S. Thomas connects the two:

It is not that he can't speak;
who created languages
but God? Nor that he won't;
to say that is to imply
malice. It is just that
he doesn't, or does so at times
when we are not listening, in
ways we have yet to recognise
as speech. We call him the dumb
God with an effrontery beyond
pardon. Whose silence so eloquent
as his? What word so explosive
as that one Palestinian
word with the endlessness of its fall-out?[7]

Notes

1 Rowan Williams, *Meeting God in Mark* (London: SPCK, 2014), p. 6.

2 Kenneth Bailey, *Jesus Through Middle Eastern Eyes: Cultural Studies in the Gospels* (London: SPCK, 2008), pp. 154–62.

3 Tom Wright, *The Day the Revolution Began: Rethinking the Meaning of Jesus' Crucifixion* (London: SPCK, 2016), p. 258; emphasis original.

4 Diarmaid MacCulloch, *Silence: A Christian History* (London: Penguin, 2014), p. 40.

5 Ibid., p. 34.

6 It isn't clear what the history of this story is: the oldest manuscripts of the Gospel lack it, and in some manuscripts it appears in different places.

7 R. S. Thomas, 'Nuclear', in *Collected Poems 1945–1990* (London: Phoenix, 1993), p. 317. Reproduced by kind permission of the Orion Publishing Group.

PART 2

The 'Negative Way'

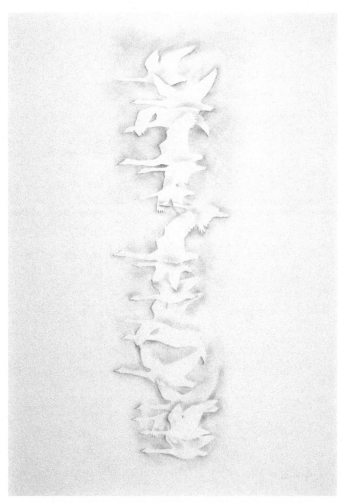

Carole Bury, 'Bewick's Swans, Returning', charcoal.

Stripping

Moses saw the bush burning ahead of him, heard his name called and responded 'Here I am.' Everything else – the discovery of his own vocational identity, the prolonged encounter, the disclosure of the name-that-is-no-name – has to wait until he stoops, loosens the binding of his shoes and steps out into his own unprotected skin.

The Song's lover, the Shulamite, has given herself body and soul to the beloved, and awaits him. When he does not come she goes to look for him, without her garment, and is forcibly stripped of her mantle.

All the Gospels recall that at his crucifixion, the soldiers took Jesus' garments from him and cast lots for them. The shock of his complete exposure, of the flesh laid bare already lacerated and broken, has been powerfully communicated in Christian art, in paintings, sculpture and film. Only in John's Gospel, though, is there an earlier scene that provides a deliberate counterpoint to this horror and supports John's distinctive reading of Jesus' Passion as his glorification:

> Jesus, knowing that the Father had given all things into his hands, and that he had come from God and was going back to God, rose from supper. He laid aside his outer garments, and taking a towel, tied it round his waist. Then he poured water into a basin and began to wash the disciples' feet. (13.3–5)[1]

This is Jesus' preparation for his suffering: it is his free choice, his action, to strip off 'all things', taking into his hands only dirty feet and water, covering himself only with a towel for others' use. The soldiers are only later able to strip him because he has already chosen to lay all things aside. As Jesus stretches to peel off his outer layer(s) during this last supper with his friends, John intends to focus our attention on Jesus' decision: the time has come to lay aside all that is unnecessary for his journey 'to God', all that might set him apart from the lowest of us.

Paul, considering the deeper identity of our Lord, turns the metaphor inside out. What is laid aside is not the 'outer garments' but everything that is held or contained within: Christ Jesus,

> though he was in the form of God, did not count equality with God a thing to be grasped, but emptied himself, taking the form of a servant, being born in the likeness of men. And being found in human form he humbled himself and became obedient unto death, even death on a cross. (Philippians 2.6–8 RSV)

Paul's image of 'emptying' (in Greek, *kenosis*), though used only this once, has had a profound impact on Christian spirituality. In this context it echoes not only the theme of 'stripping' but also Jesus' words about self-denial (Matthew 16.24; Luke 9.23).

Before we pause to explore what it all signifies, consider just one more instance of stripping. In the early third-century Roman *Apostolic Tradition* compiled by Hippolytus, we have an account of the Church's baptismal practice as he inherited it. Baptismal candidates were prepared over a three-year period, during which they received instruction and their lives were examined to see whether they were living according to the gospel; during this time they were excluded from participation with the congregation in the eucharistic liturgy. As the ceremony of baptism approached there were repeated exorcisms, fasting and an all-night vigil. The candidates strip, and there is one more exorcism, accompanied by a ceremonial anointing. Naked, they go into the water: children first, then men, then women (Hippolytus insists that they must strip everything off, even the clasps and braids that bind their hair). The baptism itself is a triple immersion, after a confession of faith in each of the Persons of the Trinity. Afterwards the newly baptized come up out of the water and are anointed again – this time an anointing not of exorcism but of thanksgiving. Finally, they robe and are admitted to the church, to another anointing, the sign of the cross on their foreheads, and to their first participation in the Eucharist.[2] Here the literal stripping naked of the candidates is the outer expression of an intense psychological and spiritual process – the repeated exorcisms signify the need to set aside layer after layer of guilt, shame and complicity in all that is wrong in the world; the lack of food and sleep free the candidates from entanglement with mundane distractions, laying bare their attention and desire. The experience of baptism would have been a momentous transition from separation to inclusion, from darkness to light, from fast to feast, from quiet and restraint to a liturgical riot of praise, scent and colour. We know that powerful memories are carried in our bodies, prompted by physical sensations: imagine how urgently and richly this sacramental experience must have been recalled whenever these people became fully present to their own bare flesh, and how resonantly the biblical imagery of stripping off must have sounded when they heard it.

By now it is abundantly clear that this stripping off isn't simply about clothes. Bare skin stands for vulnerable personal authenticity; the obstructing layers that need to come off are moral (habits and actions), volitional (desires and choices), intellectual (ideas and knowledge), psychological (patterns of thinking, and confusion about our own identities) and spiritual (the false gods uncritically imbibed from culture, and the baggage and detritus of earlier stages of our own spiritual journeys). The Christian teachers of the apophatic tradition weren't the only ones to see this; the terminology they used to express it – the Greek word *aphairesis* – was already in use in ancient philosophy and spiritual practice.

Aphairesis at its heart is simply about removing something. In maths it could refer to subtraction. In philosophy it refers to the process of abstraction – of taking away all that is unnecessary as we seek to refine a general concept (for example, the particular characteristics of individual dogs, such as straight or bandy legs, long or short hair, distinctive 'yip' or 'woof', pug or pointy nose, must all be removed in order to reach the abstract concept 'dog'). As regards God, it means removing all that gets in the way of a true understanding of divine beyondness (in other words, everything, ultimately). So there is an ambiguity here regarding *what* is being stripped. In one sense it is an idea, something purely intellectual: we start with the idea of God and then strip off all the inadequate things thought or said about it. In another sense it is each of us, a living whole: our minds and hearts and souls have to be cleared of all the lumber that gets in the way of divine meeting, stripped of all the layers that insulate our feeble flesh against the holy fire. This stripping, both of our concept of God and of our own mind, is a major theme in the fourteenth-century *Cloud of Unknowing* and *Epistle of Privy Counsel*:

> So keep a tight rein on your imagination when you offer up this naked, blind awareness of yourself to God. And make quite sure, as I am always saying, that it is naked, and not dolled up in some particular attribute of your being. For if you do 'clothe' it in some way – for example, with your own self-worthiness, or some other human or creaturely quality, then you will at once feed your imagination, and give it the opportunity and strength to drag you down to trivialities of every kind, chaotic beyond belief.[3]

Among all the complex uses of the language of stripping off, three stand out as particularly significant for the Christian apophatic tradition.

First, stripping and anointing were the familiar actions of athletes before a contest. The language of stripping thus expresses something of the disciplined preparation required of those who wish to undertake the soul's journey to God. Developing the New Testament epistles' references to athletic contests,[4] the tradition speaks of *ascesis* (which means something like a training regimen, rather less puritanical than our English word 'asceticism'). Spiritual training or discipline is frequently presented as consisting of three stages, the first being 'purgation' or 'purification', the second 'illumination' and the third 'union', although the terminology varies a little from teacher to teacher. In the first stage the moral and volitional aspects of the regimen are attended to; in the two later stages the intellectual, psychological and spiritual aspects. In all of them the Christian athlete is constantly refining his or her focus, relentlessly fixed on the one great prize. In this training regime there is both a setting aside of anything that would distract from the goal and also a progressive setting aside of earlier elements of the training that are no longer suitable. Thus among a group of athletes, some will be encouraged to do certain exercises, others discouraged from doing them, either because they are too demanding or not demanding enough. In the same way, Christian spiritual training may require us to move on beyond a certain way of praying, thinking or behaving, without in any way denying its value to others.

Second, stripping away outer layers is the activity of those who sculpt in stone or wood. With hammer and chisel the artist chips away everything extraneous to the 'true' shape that initially perhaps only they can discern in their material, so that with every blow and every loss it is more clearly revealed. The profound truth in this image is that we discover our true selves 'hidden with Christ in God' (Colossians 3.3) not by gaining new things such as virtues or knowledge but by removing or losing things. Once again, we circle back to Jesus' teaching on the paradox of spiritual life: 'Whoever finds his life will lose it, and whoever loses his life for my sake will find it' (Matthew 10.39; see also 16.25).

Third, just as the Hebrew Scriptures are full of accounts of the repeated tearing down, stripping away and clearing out from cultic high places of idolatrous altars and sacred objects, such as the trees and cedar poles sacred to Asherah, so the stripping off required of Christians is a stripping away of all the idolatrous 'baggage' that clothes their imaginations and desires. In this process we make ourselves – minds, hearts, spirits – empty, recalling Paul's language in Philippians. The baggage to be discarded is often referred to as 'thoughts' (in Greek, *logismoi*):

> What is it then to be a fool for Christ? It is to control one's thoughts when they stray out of line. It is to make the mind empty and free so as to be able to offer it in a state of readiness when Christ's teachings are to be assimilated, swept clean for the words of God that it needs to welcome.[5]

Thus the Christian negative way begins with stripping off and clearing away – not once but over and over again, in as many different ways as it takes to put into practice the command to deny ourselves and take up our crosses. Ancient athletes didn't just strip off their garments: there was a whole ritual of anointing and exfoliation, the continuing practice of removing layers of dead skin. The further we go in our journey towards divine meeting, the more we discover that means – and we will take up this topic again in the next chapter. In other ways, though, there is a sense of this being preliminary, a preparatory practice accessible to absolute beginners: the most obvious stripping off happens before the athletic contest; the boldest hammer-strokes of the artist are the first ones, with the largest lumps of matter removed. The negative way begins, similarly, with the way of 'purgation' – with the simple moral demands of the gospel: strip your heart of the idols of self, fortune, fame; learn to forgive, learn to love.

Notes

1 The word John uses is *himartia*, which might simply mean 'outer garment' (but that would be clearer if he had used the singular form *himartion*), or more generally 'clothes'. The point is, I think, not so much what Jesus removed, and how many layers there were, but the gesture itself.

2 Hippolytus deals with baptism in chapters 20 and 21 of the *Apostolic Tradition*. There is a user-friendly English version by Kevin Edgecomb available at www.bombaxo.com/hippolytus.html.

3 *Epistle of Privy Counsel* 7, translated by Clifton Wolters for Penguin Classics (London: Penguin, 1978), p. 179. The unknown author of these texts is very closely influenced by Dionysius: his works include a translation into English of *The Mystical Theology*.

4 1 Corinthians 9.24–27: 'Do you not know that in a race all the runners run, but only one receives the prize? So run that you may obtain it. Every athlete exercises self-control in all things. They do it to receive a perishable wreath, but we an imperishable. So I do not run aimlessly; I do not box as one beating the air. But I discipline my body and keep it under control, lest after preaching to others I myself should be disqualified.' Also Galatians 2.2; 5.7; Philippians 2.16; 3.14; 2 Timothy 4.7–8; Hebrews 12.1.

5 John Chrysostom, *On the Incomprehensibility of God*, sermon 5, as cited in Olivier Clément, *The Roots of Christian Mysticism* (London: New City, 1993), p. 167.

Ascent

Height and depth are almost universal metaphors for emotional and spiritual states – think, for example, of joy and despair, success and failure, clarity and confusion of mind, heaven and hell. We talk about feeling 'elevated', 'exalted' and encountering the 'sublime', or of 'feeling low', 'being brought low', 'depressed' and so on. We think of failure as a 'fall'; we knock people 'off their pedestals' or 'bring them down a rung or two'. Or we 'raise them up' as a token of success. In the highest places of all, whether Olympus, Popocatépetl, Fuji or Kailash, stories tell us that the gods abide.

Not surprisingly, therefore, many of the turning points in the Judaeo-Christian story of humanity's encounters with the divine happen in high places. It isn't just geographical mythologic that brings the ark bearing Noah's family and the survivors of the flood to rest on the top of Mount Ararat (Genesis 8.4). It also signifies God's close relationship with them: perched atop the mountain, they are high on God's heart. Abraham's trust in God is tested to the utmost, and God's loving gift of life is affirmed, in the story of the near-sacrifice/non-sacrifice of Isaac on a mountain top, Genesis 22.14 drawing from this story the proverbial moral 'On the mount of the LORD it shall be provided.' Among the varied landscapes of love's delight in the Song of Songs, the mountains are the place from which the beloved first appears and to which our gaze returns at the song's end:

The voice of my beloved!
    Behold, he comes,
leaping over the mountains,
    bounding over the hills.

41

Make haste, my beloved,
  and be like a gazelle
or a young stag
  on the mountains of spices. (2.8; 8.14)

Most importantly, the mountain top serves as the place of theophany, the place where God is seen, in three of the most important encounters of all: those of Moses, Elijah and the Transfiguration of Christ. Just as Moses was earlier told the name-that-is-no-name, so in each of these theophanies God is both seen and not seen, is simultaneously veiled and revealed.

Before we explore those theophanies it's worth pausing to recall some of the ways the image of 'ascent' fits quite intuitively with our spiritual experience. First, it is gradual. Although the conversion of the heart may be an 'all at once' experience, we work out its repercussions piecemeal over time. Faith is everywhere described as a 'journey' because we discover that over time we move our ground and the scenery changes. As we mature we add experience to the original 'deposit of faith' and it changes us – changes how we think, speak, act and pray. We learn that faithfulness does not involve circling the wagons to defend our position against attack, but willingness to step out 'beyond', following the God who goes before us.

Second, it feels like an ascent because we find ourselves not simply exchanging one scene for another but – at least sometimes – acquiring a larger perspective, being able to see how the partial glimpses that seemed so different at the time are parts of a broader landscape, being able to reconcile and integrate what earlier seemed irreconcilable. In a sense, we don't just leave a particular landscape behind as we ascend, we also leave ourselves behind, the versions of ourselves that were comfortable in the old places. In another sense, what we leave behind is God – a *version* or view of God, that is. Just as the higher up we stand, the bigger the horizon is, so too with God; as Augustine says, 'God is always greater, no matter how much we have grown.' Michael Buckley recounts a friend counselling people who have had hurtful experiences of church and family, whose comments, he says, 'come down to this: "But I am talking to you about God. And God is much bigger than this. God is really big. Really Big!"'[1]

Third, although we have to be careful not to mistake this, there is a kind of growing distance from earlier concerns: not that we cease to care about injustice or unkindness but that we are less narrow in our sympathies. Maggie Ross identifies a degree of caution about our current personal viewpoints, literally and metaphorically, as the 'basic lesson of perspective':

> Anyone who has been to Alaska or to the Russian or Mongolian steppes quickly learns how deceptive perspective can be. Mountains whose summits are 5,000 feet in elevation look like mere hills; they seem close at hand, only a mile or two distant, an easy walk, when in fact the distance is twenty or thirty miles, and the footing unstable – tussocks and muskeg, or scree, or sheer granite walls topped by knife-edge ridges.[2]

Fourth, ascent is demanding, potentially exhausting and dangerous as well as exhilarating. The higher we go, the less baggage we'll carry and the less we'll find to feed on. For good reason, most people prefer not to dwell in the heights, and as we aim for the summit we'll find fewer and fewer people alongside us. It's not for nothing that the great Old Testament prophecies of the return of the whole people to be with God called for 'every mountain and hill' to be 'made low' (Isaiah 40.4), their summits brought down to the accessible plain.

Most importantly of all, few if any of those who arrive at the summit can or should aspire to stay there; the point is nearly always to come down to the people and devote what we have seen to their service.

One final preliminary note: none of this imagery of ascent should be taken as disparaging descent. Descent is the symbol of the incarnation of Christ; the movement of descent, with its connotations of involvement with the life of creation, is the fundamental principle of kataphatic theology, and the predominant key of Christian spirituality. Both ascent and descent can be taken as involving self-abandonment, stripping and emptying, but in the context of descent these gestures tend to be for the service of others, whereas in the context of ascent they tend to be for the service of God. It won't do to see these as entirely opposed, of course.

It was on 'Horeb, the mountain of God' (Exodus 3.1) that Moses first encountered God in the burning bush. The story of Moses' ascent of the mountain to meet God in the dark cloud (Exodus 19—20) names the mountain as 'Sinai', often understood as another name for Horeb. But it is in another account of an ascent of Sinai (Exodus 33—34) that Moses daringly asks 'Show me thy glory':

> And he said, 'I will make all my goodness pass before you and will proclaim before you my name 'The LORD'. And I will be gracious to whom I will be gracious, and will show mercy on whom I will show mercy. But,' he said, 'you cannot see my face, for man shall not see me and live.' And the LORD said, 'Behold, there is a place by me where you shall stand on the rock; and while my glory passes by I will put you in a cleft of the rock, and I will cover you with my hand until I have passed by. Then I will take away my hand, and you shall see my back; but my face shall not be seen.' (33.19–23)

There follows a delightful account of spiritual sunburn: when he returns to the people, Moses' face shines so much that they are afraid (Exodus 34.30). Thereafter, in a sort of mirror image of the removal of his shoes at the burning bush, Moses needs another layer of insulation when he leaves the immediacy of divine presence: he goes veiled among the people, removing the veil whenever he returns to speak with God.

Elijah too has a triptych of mountain-top theophanies, narrated in 1 Kings 18 and 19. The first story focuses on the theme of fire: Elijah defeats the priests of Baal on Mount Carmel, calling down the fire of God. The third story places Elijah on Mount Horeb, isolated and despairing. To reach 'the mount of God', we are told, Elijah has had to spend 40 days crossing the wilderness, a journey of deprivation and exhaustion, on which he had no natural resources to sustain him – we are told that angels provided for his needs. This

44

is a negative way, a way of privation and emptying: the prophet has no company, no reassurance, no great project, no resources. Across a hostile and parched landscape he has dragged himself up to the place where Moses met with God. Did he, the great prophet of fire, imagine that God would meet him there in the drama of fire and cloud, a great unanswerable demonstration of power? Any such expectations are stripped away: God calls Elijah out of hiding, and as the prophet stands 'before the LORD':

> behold, the LORD passed by, and a great and strong wind tore the mountains and broke in pieces the rocks before the LORD, but the LORD was not in the wind. And after the wind an earthquake, but the LORD was not in the earthquake. And after the earthquake a fire, but the LORD was not in the fire. And after the fire the sound of a low whisper. (1 Kings 19.11–12)

Wind, earthquake and fire are all elsewhere acceptable symbols of divine power and presence, but here on Horeb, Elijah encounters presence-in-emptiness. At this point in his story, Elijah feels (wrongly, as God points out) that he is the only follower of the LORD left alive – and only just alive; the weight of the whole history of God's love for humanity seems to rest on his shoulders. Alastair Redfern comments:

> For the prophet, the guardian of this precious and formative inheritance, God is not revealed in these spectacular places – he is known in the still-small voice – in the silence of a heart crying out for salvation. This is a deeper, more personal encounter – sometimes translated as 'sheer silence'.[3]

A voice which is no-voice demonstrates the power that is no-power, an apophatic counterweight to the theology of fire-and-violence in the first of our Elijah triptych.

In the middle episode of the triptych we are on Mount Carmel, in the immediate aftermath of the fire incident. Famine, with all its attendant evils, has an iron grip on the land: the prophet's task is to intervene for rain on behalf of a desperate people. Elijah pronounces that he hears 'the sound of the rushing of rain', and goes to the mountain top to pray.

And he said to his servant, 'Go up now, look towards the sea.' And he went up and looked and said, 'There is nothing.' And he said, 'Go again,' seven times. And at the seventh time he said, 'Behold, a little cloud like a man's hand is rising from the sea' . . . And in a little while the heavens grew black with clouds and wind, and there was a great rain. (1 Kings 18.43–45)

The jewel at the heart of this little story has been polished to brilliance in the work of the sixteenth-century Spanish poet-priest and Doctor of the Church, St John of the Cross. A friar in the Carmelite order, which takes Elijah as its founder, John wrote *The Ascent of Mount Carmel*, a treatise on the soul's ascent to God. He produced a little sketch as a summary of the work, a picture of Mount Carmel, with what appear to be three paths towards the height. One path is that of the 'goods of earth', another the 'goods of heaven': both are annotated 'the more I desired to seek them, the less I had.' Both appear to be dead ends. A third way leads up to the 'honour and glory of God'. Here John has written simply: 'nothing nothing nothing nothing nothing nothing and even on the Mount nothing' – seven nothings, echoing the seven reports of Elijah's servant. An explanatory verse is added, filling all the blank space available at the base of the sketch; some of its lines have already been quoted (in the Introduction). Here are the opening lines:

To reach satisfaction in all
　　desire satisfaction in nothing.
To come to the knowledge of all
　　desire the knowledge of nothing.
To come to possess all
　　desire the possession of nothing.
To arrive at being all
　　desire to be nothing.

This is John's great theme of *todo y nada*, the All and the Nothing. Elijah's apophatic encounters become the standard for all who seek God. Whatever it is that is heard is also beyond hearing; whatever it is that is seen is also beyond seeing. Fire and rain sometimes appear but God is not to be sought in them. Desire is the pivot, and by a sort of grammatical sleight of hand, 'do not desire anything' becomes 'desire nothing', desire to encounter the no-thing that is God, desire to be wholly the no-thing that we are by comparison with God. In his poem *The Dark Night*, John sees that God is 'no one':

One dark night,
filled with love's urgent longings
ah, the sheer grace ! –
I went out unseen . . .
to where he was awaiting me
him I knew so well –
there in a place where no one appeared.[4]

John's careful dissection of the spiritual ascent challenges much that we take for granted. We are usually inclined, for example, to desire the 'goods of heaven' – his list includes 'glory', 'joy', 'knowledge', 'consolation' and 'rest' – but for John they are no better, ultimately, than the 'goods of earth' (in both cases, although the desire to possess them is self-defeating, he affirms that when one ceases to desire them, one has them all 'without desire'). John has harsh words for those who are satisfied with the kind of religious observance that identifies us as 'Christian' in the world's eyes and our own:

Oh, who can make this counsel of our Savior understandable, and practicable, and attractive that spiritual persons might become aware of the difference between the method many of them think is good and that which ought to be used in traveling this road! They are of the opinion that any kind of withdrawal from the world or reformation of life suffices. Some are content with a certain degree of virtue, perseverance in prayer, and mortification but never achieve the nakedness, poverty, selflessness, or spiritual purity (which are all the same) about which the Lord counsels us here. For they still feed and clothe their natural selves with spiritual feelings and consolations instead of divesting and denying themselves of these for God's sake. They think a denial of self in worldly matters is sufficient without an annihilation and purification of spiritual possessions. It happens that, when some of this solid, perfect food (the annihilation of all sweetness in God – the pure spiritual cross and nakedness of Christ's poverty of spirit) is offered them in dryness, distaste, and trial, they run from it as from death and wander about in search only of sweetness and delightful communications from God. Such an attitude is not the hallmark of self-denial and nakedness of spirit but the indication of a spiritual sweet tooth. Through this kind of conduct they become, spiritually speaking, enemies of the cross of Christ. (Philippians 3.18)[5]

John draws devastatingly accurate portraits of types who revel in the latest spiritual fads and fashions; few of us will emerge entirely unscathed from reading them. Once we see the dangers of religiosity we will realize that the ascent is not simply a natural process of growth into maturity but requires active and determined measures. The author of *The Cloud of Unknowing*, writing two centuries or so before John, talks repeatedly of the need to 'trample' on our thoughts, even when they are apparently holy.[6] The image is a helpful one: in order to trample on something, we need to stand on it, and as we trample on it, it bears our weight and gives us a footing that can lift us up to take our next steps – 'trample' and 'trampoline' come from the same Germanic root.

John's discussion of the soul's ascent is not a treatise for a theological textbook: he is writing as spiritual guide and confessor to women and men who are actively engaged in the spiritual life. They are not learning 'about' the way in theory; they are on it, and they look to him as guide. Contemporary readers sometimes describe John's advice as severe and off-putting, but he is gentle, and his focus on the difficulties along the way is a response to the questions and difficulties of those he advised. The ascent to God is a way of prayer, liturgy, devotion and practical work. But it is also thoroughgoingly apophatic: if we are to ascend to holy encounter, it is by way of stripping and the passage through the dark nights of the soul, about which John writes from experience with originality and deep insight. He turns the three great Christian virtues of faith, hope and love into instruments of apophasis: faith empties the mind of all that has been seen, turning it towards the unseen (Hebrews 11.1); hope empties the memory of what is past and orientates it towards the future; love empties the will of all other affections and turns it towards the beloved.[7] John reminds us that the Ark of the Covenant was empty: this is a sign of what we must be if God is to dwell in us.[8] None of this is to be taken in a nihilistic sense; it is the very opposite of life-denying. John was a man who enjoyed natural beauty and delighted in poetry, song and dance; he was a practical man who loved to build and garden. All of life is glorious; but even so, is nothing by comparison with God.

With the acumen of a great spiritual director, John has seen how much of our spirituality is rooted in self-love rather than self-abandon. Our religious experiences, our charismatic gifts, our spiritual exercises and even our suffering are only idols if they are at the service of the self. Better to cast them all aside:

A genuine spirit seeks the distasteful in God rather than the delectable, leans more toward suffering than toward consolation, more toward going without everything for God than toward possession. It prefers dryness and affliction to sweet consolation. It knows that this is the significance of following Christ and denying self, that the other method is perhaps a seeking of self in God – something entirely contrary to love. Seeking oneself in God is the same as looking for the caresses and consolations of God. Seeking God in oneself entails not only the desire of doing without these consolations for God's sake but also the inclination to choose for love of Christ all that is most distasteful whether in God or in the world; and this is what loving God means.[9]

On top of Horeb/Sinai, both Moses and Elijah met with the God who is beyond meeting, the God whose infinite transcendence so intoxicatingly sweeps away the barrier between presence and absence. On top of an unnamed 'high mountain' they are seen together in conversation with Jesus, in the last of our theophanies, recorded in Matthew 17.1–8, Mark 9.2–8 and Luke 9.28–36. Once again, faces shine brightly and God is present in dazzling cloud. Jesus is revealed 'in his glory'. He is the Word, to whom the disciples must listen. He is lowest and highest, beginning and end, broken and whole, finite and infinite: in the radiance of this visionary encounter, disciples catch a glimpse of the fullness of divinity in a human heart emptied of all but love. In the apophatic tradition, the significance of the Transfiguration is not to set Jesus apart from us by the demonstration that he alone unites divinity and humanity, but quite the opposite: this is how he saves us, by showing us the way of self-emptying. For Carmelites, Christ is not only 'the Way' but the mountain itself: the higher we ascend, the deeper we go into identification with him.

In the next chapter we will see what one of John's predecessors in the apophatic tradition made of this encounter. For now we might muse over how he might have responded to these words from a very different figure, Rainer Maria Rilke, on the need not merely to be witnesses of the Transfiguration but agents of it:

> How all things are in migration! How they seek refuge in us. How each of them desires to be relieved of externality and to live again in the Beyond which we enclose and deepen within ourselves. We are convents of lived things, dreamed things, impossible things ... Little cemeteries that we are, adorned with the flowers of our futile gestures, containing so many corpses that demand that we testify to their souls. All prickly with crosses, all covered with inscriptions, all spaded up and shaken by countless daily burials, we are charged with the transmutation, the resurrection, the transfiguration of all things. For how can we save what is visible if not by using the language of absence, of the invisible? And how to speak this language that remains mute unless we sing it with abandon and without any insistence on being understood.
>
> Letter to Sophy Giauque
> 26 November 1925[10]

Notes

1 Augustine, 'Expositions on the Psalms' 63, cited in Michael J. Buckley, SJ, *What Do You Seek? The Questions of Jesus as Challenge and Promise* (Grand Rapids, MI: Eerdmans, 2016), p. 129. The reference to his friend Tom Weston's spiritual advice is on the same page.

2 Maggie Ross, *Silence: A User's Guide* (London: Darton, Longman & Todd, 2014), p. 135.

3 Alastair Redfern, *The Leadership of the People of God: A Study of I and II Kings* (Delhi: ISPCK, 2013), pp. 64–5.

4 *The Dark Night*, stanzas 1 and 4, quoting Kieran Kavanaugh's translation in *John of the Cross: Doctor of Light and Love* for the Crossroad Spiritual Legacy series (New York: Crossroad, 1999), pp. 29, 31.

5 *Ascent of Mount Carmel* 2.7.5, quoting Kieran Kavanaugh's translation in *John of the Cross: Selected Writings* for the Classics of Western Spirituality series (New York: Paulist Press, 1987), pp. 94–5.

6 For example, *The Cloud of Unknowing* 7, translated by Clifton Wolters for Penguin Classics (London: Penguin, 1978), p. 68.

7 *Ascent of Mount Carmel* 2.6.1, in Kavanaugh (1987), pp. 92–3.

8 *Ascent of Mount Carmel* 1.5.7, in Kavanaugh (1987), p. 92.

9 *Ascent of Mount Carmel* 2.7.5, in Kavanaugh (1987), p. 95.

10 http://yearwithrilke.blogspot.co.uk/2011/06/charged-with-trans figuration-of-all.

Unsaying

A few years ago, Ford UK had a television/online advertising campaign running. Through a series of snapshots they reminded us how we have in recent years completely changed our assumptions about postal deliveries, old age pensioners, drivers and more. The punchline: Unlearn Everything. Let Go of What You Know. A quick internet search on the topic of 'unlearning' confirms that there is a great deal of interest in this approach to knowledge. Its theoretical basis is at least partly in the groundbreaking work of Thomas Kuhn, summed up in his 1962 book *The Structure of Scientific Revolutions*. Kuhn showed that we don't acquire knowledge as we might build a tower, first laying the foundations and then building on them, each layer supported by earlier learning; even during periods of time while this does seem to be what's happening, we are in fact steadily accumulating ideas that won't fit into the current structure, ideas that we set aside like bricks that are too oddly shaped to be of use. Periodically what we need to do is knock down the structure we've been working on, taking the bricks and rebuilding something quite different, into which all those previously ill-fitting ideas can now be incorporated – indeed, they might be among the most important building-blocks.

Two hundred years before Kuhn an even more powerful challenge to the traditional understanding of knowledge was issued by the Christian philosopher Immanuel Kant. Kant showed how deeply and incorrigibly our understanding is coloured by our own perspectives, capacities and histories. If one philosophical argument could be credited with putting an end to the era of modernity and ushering in postmodernity, it would probably be this one (though it had a long fuse). Kant showed that all we can ever know is how things appear to us, how they are interpreted by minds like ours, not how they are in themselves.

52

It's fascinating to see contemporary culture applying to all kinds of knowledge the apophatic tradition's core message about God: don't mistake your view of a thing for the thing itself. However initially helpful, your view will eventually get in your way. But with all due respect to postmen, old age pensioners, drivers and scientists, the apophatic tradition's approach is both similar to and different from the contemporary interest in unlearning. Both agree that what we currently say or think (whether about postmen or about God) says at least as much about who we are (our interests, language, perspective and so on) as about the object. Both agree that in order to make progress towards reality and truth we will sometimes – even for quite long periods – be working steadily on digesting, applying and incrementally adding to what we already believe to be true, while at other times there will be a potentially cataclysmic realization that it is all too deeply flawed and just needs to go. For both there will be times – exciting or terrifying – when we are vulnerably 'in-between', unsure of what to think or say, unanchored and adrift.

In the apophatic tradition, just as in any branch of understanding, therefore, there needs to be a regular, repeated practice of unsaying, unlearning, unknowing. We put aside 'childish things' (1 Corinthians 13.11); we acquire new perspectives that challenge old views; we learn new languages, with new ways of seeing and saying embedded within them. Each new element has positive value, enabling us to see more widely; but that value is limited, and when we have wrung everything we can from it, it will at some stage need to give way to something else.

However, the fundamental difference springs from the fact that talk about God is not talk about one aspect of reality, one item or class of things distinguished from others. When we talk about the divine source, the infinite beyond, there is a more profound inadequacy in our words. In a sense there is no improvement as we swap one idea for another. From our perspective, certainly, some ideas about God are 'higher' than others. From the divine perspective, however, all are so far from the truth that none describes it 'better' than others. That's why the Church continues to be happy to use such baby-pictures as Jesus' feet disappearing into the clouds at his Ascension, and countless Christians give a hospitable welcome to Santa Claus. These simple images have a positive value utterly unlike the nostalgic charm of outdated scientific ideas.[1]

Apophasis is a learning process, a conversation. It doesn't take the words from our mouths before we can say them. Apophatic negation is the kind of erasure of meaning that looks like, not like a vacuum. Holy silence comes in, through and after the words; it does not seek to abort them. We speak about the divine because the divine creates our world by and through and in speech. There is a rhythm to it: saying and unsaying. It is the rhythm of ascent: planting feet, then lifting them. We pour meaning into words and watch as it overflows beyond them.

The Song of Songs' language of touch, taken up in so many Christian writers, gives us a helpful way of saying this. The problem for any object of thought is that even when we grasp it, we can only say what it is like in and to our grasp – whereas when it comes to the divine, we can touch or be touched but cannot *comprehend*, cannot enclose the divine in our fist, cannot get our hands to circle it or our 'heads around it'. The distinct impression we get is that it's the other way around: we are in God's grasp, he comprehends us. God simply won't be 'an object of thought': it's not in the power of the dividing and distinguishing intellect but in the power of desiring, tentative, unifying love, to approach the divine.

Growth in knowledge about mundane things may involve regular unsaying but it does not undermine the process of talking itself. Talk about divinity, on the other hand, confounds speech, liquidizes it. Michael Sells demonstrates:

The formal denial that the transcendent can be named must in some sense be valid, otherwise ineffability would not become an issue. Insofar as it is valid, however, the formal statement of ineffability turns back upon itself, and undoes itself. To say 'X is beyond names', if true, entails that it cannot then be called by the name 'X'. In turn, the statement 'it cannot be called X' becomes suspect, since the 'it', as a pronoun, substitutes for a name, but the transcendent is beyond all names . . . I am caught in a linguistic regress. Each statement I make – positive or 'negative' – reveals itself as in need of correction. The correcting statement must then itself be corrected, ad infinitum. The authentic subject of discourse slips continually back beyond each effort to name it or even to deny its nameability.[2]

So whereas scientists and philosophers might continually need to refine, refurbish and replace their existing ideas and interpretations with improved versions, recognizing that they will never have a complete and final 'theory of everything', apophatic theologians add to their iterative discipline of saying and unsaying a more radical move 'away from speech' altogether. The 'ascent through negations', taking step by step all the positive affirmations we might make of God, and unsaying each of them, leads to a silence where all speech has been put away. Moses at the summit of Sinai awaits the cloudy presence of God. The Shulamite ceases her Song.

One of the great spiritual gifts of the Jewish tradition is its recognition that divine 'truth' is not something we're supposed to accept passively. The great patriarchs take the risk of arguing with God; Abram's wife Sarai even laughs at his words. The story of what happened to Jacob at the Ford of Jabbok dramatically expresses what it feels like to engage in the process of unsaying. Jacob is on a dangerous journey, back to an encounter with the brother whose birthright he stole. He makes himself completely vulnerable, sending his whole company ahead of him across the ford.

> And Jacob was left alone. And a man wrestled with him until the breaking of the day. When the man saw that he did not prevail against Jacob, he touched his hip socket, and Jacob's hip was put out of joint as he wrestled with him. Then he said, 'Let me go, for the day has broken.' But Jacob said, 'I will not let you go unless you bless me.' And he said to him, 'What is your name?' And he said, 'Jacob.' Then he said, 'Your name shall no longer be called Jacob, but Israel, for you have striven with God and with men, and have prevailed.' Then Jacob asked him, 'Please tell me your name.' But he said, 'Why is it that you ask my name?' And there he blessed him. So Jacob called the name of the place Peniel, saying, 'For I have seen God face to face, and yet my life has been delivered.' (Genesis 32.24–30)

The expectation that we will wrestle with God is admittedly not always to the fore in the Hebrew Scriptures, though it is particularly resonant in many Psalms which, as is often pointed out, were 'Jesus' hymn-book'. Nor is it a dominant theme of the New Testament as a whole. Nevertheless, it is plainly there in Jesus' own treatment of Scripture and in his characteristic use of teaching methods such as parable and hyperbole, which resist interpretation and force us to wrestle meaning from them (Mark 4.11–12). We might further discern it being performed for us as the Evangelists shape their inheritance of faith into four distinctive perspectives on Christ's identity and work, and the writers of letters shape their messages to very different congregations.

So if you think that unsaying sounds fairly undemanding, then you haven't yet understood what it involves. Stripping, ascending and unsaying *can* be as easy as laying aside a sweater on a warm day, a stroll on a gentle gradient or just choosing a different set of words – but not always. Like the poor lover being beaten and stripped of her garment, like a mountaineer clinging by the fingertips to a crumbling rock-face, those who practise unsaying will find themselves at times vulnerable and alone, struggling against something that chokes and cripples. The contest is exhausting and painful. Those who follow the apophatic path can feel as if they are continually having to fight against their own faith, being thrown, losing their grip, losing faith daily in order to find it anew again. They can be isolated among a believing community that does not share their sense that God is beyond their current understanding. In more violent times, many mystics were burnt at the stake.

Yet at some point it may dawn on us that in our struggle we are actually held by God and that there is a transformative blessing in it. The wounding and the blessing go together. And the struggle turns out to be our most fundamental and characteristic practice, because this is what it *means* to be 'Israel': 'one who strives with God'.

Wrestling with language to make it point beyond itself to the unsayable, we say and unsay.

This is not always in the pantomime pattern of affirmation and negation: 'Oh yes it is'; 'Oh no it isn't'. The smallest phrase can undo itself: the divine encounter is described as 'dazzling darkness', as 'sober drunkenness'. These apparent contradictions are not quite nonsense: they still convey something or convey us somewhere. They are not simply apophatic correctives to the otherwise steady flow of kataphatic theology, but exert a disruptive force within that flow. Once you have stubbed your toes on 'dazzling darkness' you might be more cautious as you approach something like 'Heavenly Father' or 'spiritual power'.

Nor is saying and unsaying about God a kind of thesis and antithesis, two contradictory elements that can be reconciled into a higher synthesis. Synthetic theology is not apophatic. There is admittedly a similarity in that after we have affirmed, for example, that 'God is our Father' and 'God is not our Father', we usually frame a higher truth that contains something of the truth of both: 'God is our Father in a spiritual sense.' This is the truth of ascent. However, the point of the saying and unsaying is not to seek a higher reconciliation but to allow the tension between the two to tear the veil of language apart for a moment and allow us a glimpse of the beyond. Denys Turner explains:

> we must say affirmatively that God is 'light', and then say, denying this, that God is 'darkness'; and finally we must 'negate the negation' between darkness and light, which we do by saying 'God is a brilliant darkness'. For the negation of the negation is not a *third* utterance, additional to the affirmative and the negative, in good linguistic order; it is not some intelligible *synthesis* of affirmation and negation; it is rather the collapse of our affirmation and denials into disorder, which we can only express, *a fortiori*, in bits of collapsed, disordered language . . .[3]

Apophatic language is as out of joint as Jacob's hip: it goes limpingly.

The apophatic theologian has two basic strategies to work with: the first is to use ordinary speech of God, kataphasis, and then to unsay it; the second is to find ways of speaking that unsay themselves. Among this second type are paradox and 'collapsed language' of many kinds, including one dazzling contribution from the seventh-century Constantinopolitan writer Maximus the Confessor.

During the early centuries of the Church, Christ's followers were working out the implications of their faith on the hoof; theology was not divided into the neat compartments implied in later textbooks. So the apophatic tradition developed hand in hand with the kataphatic. Gregory of Nyssa, for example, was a key figure in the development not only of apophatic but also of Trinitarian theology. In the life and work of Maximus, similarly, apophatic theology is inseparable from theological investigation into the nature of Christ and of humanity, and from practical advice for disciples.

At the fourth-century Council of Nicaea, Christ was asserted to be both human and divine. How to explain the paradox of one person being both mortal and immortal, changing and unchanging, growing in knowledge and yet all-knowing, in time and beyond time was the stuff of controversy for the centuries that followed.

Maximus' genius was to see that the relationship between kataphasis and apophasis, and between the humanity and the divinity of Christ, are connected because both come from the same source: they are both 'theophanies', disclosures of God.[4] So Maximus roots an account of kataphasis and apophasis in a discussion of the greatest theophany of the New Testament: the Transfiguration of Christ. Here both the humanity and the divinity of Christ are revealed, and Maximus draws a parallel between, on the one hand, the incarnation of the Word in flesh and in human words, and on the other hand the transcendent divinity, 'his invisible infinity', which cannot be captured in word or thought.[5] He spells it out in a marvellous and gently humorous reflection known in my household as the 'Fat Jesus/Thin Jesus lesson':

> In the active person the Word grows fat by the practice of the virtues and becomes flesh. In the contemplative it grows lean by spiritual understandings and becomes as it was in the beginning, God the Word . . .
> The one who speaks of God in positive affirmations is making the Word flesh. Making use only of what can be seen and felt

he knows God as their cause. But the one who speaks of God negatively through negations is making the Word spirit, as in the beginning he was God and with God. Using absolutely nothing which can be known he knows in a better way the utterly Unknowable.[6]

It is one of the great delights of Maximus' theology that he binds speech and action so fully together. Positive talk about God is inseparable from action in accordance with the commandments: both put flesh on the bones of faith, making God known in the world. Unsaying and personal ascesis are equally inseparable: both strip everything back, directing our attention to the beyond. More than any other theologian of this tradition, Maximus sees a continuity between the denials of apophasis and the self-denial that is the way of the cross.

But to return to Jesus, whose divinity and humanity are neither all mixed up to make a god–man hybrid nor segregated by a sort of psychological apartheid: the emerging consensus of the Church was that these two distinct natures were fully present to one another, mutually interpenetrating, so that we can truly say that in Christ, humanity comes to dwell in the Godhead and the Godhead in humanity. There is a flow, in other words – activities that might otherwise be characteristic only of God are now found in humanity and vice versa.

Maximus pushes the point home: there is a similar flow between positive and negative theologies. When we use words to point to what is beyond – words such as 'beyond being', for example – we deny that they can be used of humanity. When we take a word and deny that it is true of humanity – a word such as 'lifeless', for example – we can use it in a transcendent sense to describe the God who is both 'superbeing' and 'nonbeing'. When we take a word and affirm it of humanity – a word such as 'living', for example – we must deny its application to the beyond.[7] Thus saying and unsaying weave in and out of one another; things we might once have hesitated to say can now be said, and things we have loved to say are now to be denied.

For all the technical jargon and the beautifully complex analysis that can be built on the back of the apophatic tradition, Maximus reverently brings us back to the core: this is about how we know God, and is the shape stamped on our speech by Jesus, the incarnate 'image of the invisible God' (Colossians 1.15), and his cross.

Notes

1 This insight is more fully developed in the Dionysian corpus' notion of 'unlike likenesses' of God – see chapter III.2.

2 Michael A. Sells, *Mystical Languages of Unsaying* (Chicago: Chicago University Press, 1994), p. 2.

3 Denys Turner, *The Darkness of God: Negativity in Christian Mysticism* (Cambridge: Cambridge University Press, 1995), p. 22.

4 Maximus may be building on a hint contained in the Fourth Letter ascribed to Dionysius the Areopagite.

5 Maximus the Confessor, *Ambiguum 10* 1165D–1168A, translated by Nicholas Constas, in *On Difficulties in the Church Fathers: The Ambigua*, Vol. 1 (Cambridge, MA: Harvard University Press, 2014), pp. 267–9.

6 Maximus the Confessor, *Chapters on Knowledge* II.37, 39, translated by George Berthold in the Classics of Western Spirituality Series, *Maximus the Confessor: Selected Writings* (New York: Paulist Press, 1985), p. 156.

7 This theme of the 'flip-flop' nature of our language about Christ and about God is frequent in Maximus. A good example is in the 'Introduction' to *The Church's Mystagogy*, also included in the Classics of Western Spirituality volume (p. 185).

Union

Christians follow the tradition of the Jews in proclaiming that 'The Lord our God is one.' Monotheism is about much more than an argument over how many gods we can count. If the oneness of God were just the numerical one-as-opposed-to-several, then to say that 'God is one' wouldn't tell us very much about what kind of God this is, simply that there aren't any others. Theology explores other kinds of unity that do tell us about the nature of God, such as *simplicity*, not in the everyday sense of 'easy to understand' but in its philosophical sense, meaning 'not a composite of parts'. God isn't *partial* in the sense of 'loving to some but not others', or in the sense of 'partly loving but partly wrathful'. Whatever God is, God is completely, all the way through. In contemporary parlance, words like *integral* probably capture this sense better. This means, of course, that biblical comments about God 'changing his mind' and so on have to be read as anthropomorphic metaphors, just as we read comments about 'the arm of the LORD' or 'the mouth of the LORD'.

The simplicity of God, however, does not mean that God is bland and one-dimensional: the doctrine of the Trinity requires us to think of unity in diversity. Ancient philosophers and spiritual writers puzzled obsessively over the question of how a cosmos could start with One pure spirit and degenerate into Many divided and warring beings, spiritual and material, impure and subject to decay. The Christian response begins from the insight that 'God is Love' (1 John 4.8), which means that divine oneness is active and loving unity. Therefore 'otherness' is not a problem to be fended off but integral to divine life, because love creates relationship out of difference.

How we talk about divine oneness matters tremendously. The 'One God' can become the ultimate dictator, legitimating suppression of difference in his name by political and spiritual authorities; 'Our Father' becomes the lynchpin of earthly patriarchy. This is one reason why the apophatic tradition is often more comfortable saying that God is 'nothing' than that God is 'one'. 'One' can be such a sticky concept, to which our projected fantasies of power and identity cling like barnacles; 'nothing' chops them off abruptly, reminding us that God is beyond everything definable as a 'this' or 'that'. To say that God is 'no-thing' is a way of challenging ourselves, asking whether anything in our language of 'one' is another covering that needs to go, another idea that needs to be trampled on in our ascent to God.

For all that, we nevertheless remain monotheists, and the language of 'one' can be used apophatically if it is read carefully and inclusively (and denied when necessary). The One God leaves no 'other' beyond him but creates all things, remains in all things and draws all things back towards him in love. God's activity is described by Julian of Norwich as 'onyng', *making one*; this is the central prayer of Jesus' extended farewell to his disciples:

> I do not ask for these only, but also for those who will believe in me through their word, that they may all be one, just as you, Father, are in me, and I in you, that they also may be in us, so that the world may believe that you have sent me. The glory that you have given me I have given to them, that they may be one even as we are one, I in them and you in me, that they may become perfectly one. (John 17.20–23)

So the soul in its ascent to God is becoming less split apart, more at peace with itself and others; this healthy growth towards integration is one meaning of 'salvation'. The process of 'onyng' is continuous: we are becoming one with others and ourselves at the same time as we are becoming one with Christ, and growing into his oneness with the Father. (Ironically, as we grow in capacity to be at peace with those who are 'other' than us, we often find ourselves held in suspicion by our 'own' people. Until we grow in unity as communities, the call of the God who makes us one can be experienced as painful and divisive, as Jesus warned – see Mark 13.12.)

In earlier chapters we have pondered the two most powerful images of the soul's destination in God: Moses enveloped in the shining cloud of the presence of God atop Sinai, and the Shulamite lover in the darkness of her chamber. Both these images can suggest that the event of encounter is utterly different from the ascent to it, as different as darkness is from light or absence is from presence. This way of speaking about the soul's union with God can be helpful, but it too can distract and mislead if it becomes detached from an understanding of the entire Christian life as an integrative process.

Because God is One, then everything we have to do with God is about oneness; union doesn't suddenly start at the summit of the spiritual life. There is a kind of union with God that is simply a precondition of life: without God's intimate presence to us, we could not exist at all. As Job's young friend Elihu reminds him:

> The spirit of God has made me,
>   and the breath of the Almighty gives me life.
> If he should set his heart to it
>   and gather to himself his spirit and his breath,
> all flesh would perish together,
>   and man would return to dust. (Job 33.4; 34.14–15)

Talk about union becomes fully apophatic when we make it clear we are talking about a union *beyond* union of thought and will, a more radical union in the literal sense: one that digs deeper into our roots in God.

In discussing the apophatic ascent we admired Maximus the Confessor's account of the Transfiguration. Maximus also offers an entrancingly holistic account of the human soul as a microcosm, a miniature version of the cosmos, in which all divisions are progressively healed. He identifies five 'divisions' or chasms that mar the unity of all things: between God and creation; between the world of the mind and the world of the senses; between heaven and earth; between paradise and the earth we inhabit; between male and female. One by one, starting with gender division and working upwards, the work of grace in the soul is to knit fractures together:

This is why man was introduced last among beings – like a kind of natural bond mediating between the universal extremes through his parts, and unifying through himself things that by nature are separated from each other by a great distance – so that, by making of his own division a beginning of the unity which gathers up all things to God their Author . . . he might reach the limit of the sublime ascent that comes about through the union of all things in God, in whom there is no division . . .[1]

Maximus is commenting here on the Christian belief that in the life and work of Christ, human nature is 'divinized' by being brought fully within the Trinitarian life of God. This is why the unifying work of salvation does not stop at healing all the divisions within creation but extends further, bridging the divide between creation and God. Maximus describes this final stage in the soul's 'onyng' in slightly wistful terms: if only we had not fallen, this is what we were created for, but owing to the Fall it has instead been accomplished for us and in us by Christ.

[H]ad man united created nature with the uncreated through love (oh, the wonder of God's love for mankind!), he would have shown them to be one and the same by the state of grace, the whole man wholly pervading the whole God, and becoming everything that God is, without, however, identity in essence, and receiving the whole of God instead of himself, and obtaining as a kind of prize for his ascent to God the absolutely unique God . . .[2]

The soul's union with God, which is the summit of the most arduous of journeys, the way of the cross to the world and the self, is also in another sense a return to what we were originally created to be and always have been within the loving heart of God.

We noted earlier that Christian spiritual teachers have often divided the soul's journey to God into three stages: purification, illumination and union. In the stage of illumination the soul gains knowledge of God and progresses through learning and unlearning, saying and unsaying, serially trying on and then stripping off all the teachings of the tradition. In the third stage, as in this poem from St John of the Cross, the soul moves beyond knowledge:

I entered into unknowing
and there I remained unknowing
transcending all knowledge.

I entered into unknowing,
yet when I saw myself there,
without knowing where I was,
I understood great things;
I will not say what I felt
for I remained unknowing
transcending all knowledge.

That perfect knowledge
was of peace and holiness
held at no remove [understood directly]
in profound solitude;
it was something so secret
that I was left stammering,
transcending all knowledge.

I was so 'whelmed,
so absorbed and withdrawn,
that my senses were left
deprived of all their sensing,
and my spirit was given
an understanding while not understanding,
transcending all knowledge.[3]

Like sight, knowledge depends on an element of duality. Grammar distinguishes the 'knower' from 'the object of knowledge'. Aside from the fact that the Creator of all cannot *be* any kind of 'object', the divine activity of 'onyng' finally removes the ground from under any duality. The soul's 'solitude' is not necessarily a denial of divine presence; when it is united with God, there are not two beings to count. Peace and holiness are 'held at no remove', as John says. In so far as the soul speaks at all there, it stammers, tripping itself up, disrupting its own saying.

Apophatic teachers therefore use the language of unknowing to mean something that is the opposite of blank ignorance. It signifies both an emptiness, an absence of anything that the mind can catch and hold on to, and also a fullness or excess – the heart and mind so filled with the vivid and dynamic life of God that there is no space or time left over as a ground for observation. The cloud of unknowing is not the same thing as God or union; it is a place of vulnerability where the divine *may* meet us. The beloved is sometimes present in the Shulamite's chamber but sometimes there is only crushing absence there. We may climb to the top of the mountain but we can't make God be there for us: that is a matter for grace. The old usage of 'knowing' to convey sexual intimacy – as for example in Genesis 4.1, 'Now Adam knew Eve his wife, and she conceived' – is subverted: the more intimate encounter leaves no space for knowledge. As the author of *The Cloud of Unknowing* explains:

> Therefore I will leave on one side everything I can think, and choose for my love that thing which I cannot think! Why? Because he may well be loved, but not thought. By love he can be caught and held, but by thinking never. Therefore, though it may be good sometimes to think particularly about God's kindness and worth, and though it may be enlightening too, and a part of contemplation, yet in the work now before us it must be put down and covered with a cloud of forgetting. And you are to step over it resolutely and eagerly, with a devout and kindling love, and try to penetrate that darkness above you. Strike that thick cloud of unknowing with the sharp dart of longing love, and on no account whatever think of giving up.[4]

Speaking about the union of the soul with God is both paradoxical – we are speaking of the ineffable – and dangerous. Dangerous, first, because as soon as it is in words it is terribly seductive. Union can so easily become our ambition. Why would we not seek it? Because it is God we must seek, not for our own sake, not to get anything from him. Over and over again, contemplative guides identify this spiritual ambition as the last and worst temptation of the soul. We must strip off every trace of ego, every last layer of self-interest, until there is no 'me' left in our approach to God.

Speaking about union is dangerous also because it is easy to misunderstand. The textbooks on mysticism, and the history of the Church's decisions about 'heresy', are full of stark warnings that union cannot mean the erasure of the fundamental distinction of 'nature' or 'substance' between humanity and divinity. When we come to worship, it won't do to be confused about who is God and who is not! I hope that the inadequacy of the language of nature and substance will become clear in later chapters; for now, we should perhaps just hold fast to Mother Julian's understanding of God's oneness as the activity of 'onyng': not of obliterating difference but of bringing difference into unity.

Apophatic texts are often difficult to read, not only because of the grammatical difficulty of talking about a God who is not a stable 'object of discourse', and not only because the writers are fiercely intent on stopping us reifying and idolizing their subject matter. More significantly, they're difficult because they are not intended as *descriptions* of the way up to divine encounter, rather they are intended to push us towards it. To put it another way, they are not so much telling us about the apophatic journey as prompting it to happen by performing the gesture of pointing away from speech. When you read the works of the apophatic tradition, if you put them down and say 'that was interesting', they have failed in their intent. As Michael Sells says:

> apophatic language attempts to evoke in the reader an event that is – in its movement beyond structures of self and other, subject and object – structurally analogous to the event of mystical union ... Unsaying ... demands a willingness to let go, at a particular moment, of the grasping for guarantees and for knowledge as a possession. It demands a moment of vulnerability. Yet for those who value it, this moment of unsaying and unknowing is what it is to be human.[5]

The point is to keep finding yourself sliding off the pages into prayer or action or focused awareness; or waking up to find that you have been lost in divine arms. The paradoxical logic of union is that in losing ourselves in the divine, we find out what it is to be human.

A curious place in the apophatic tradition is held by the thirteenth-century Frenchwoman Marguerite Porete, author of *The Mirror of Simple Souls*. The souls to whom it is dedicated are 'simple' in both senses of the word: both those outside the educated and clerical elite, and those in whom the work of spiritual integration is already underway. Porete's work was condemned and she was burnt as a heretic. Bernard McGinn underlines the significance: 'Marguerite is the first documented case of an execution for mystical heresy in Western Christianity ... Unfortunately, it was not to be the last.'[6] In her case the danger of wielding the apophatic language of union, and especially of doing so in a way that is accessible to ordinary people, is made terribly clear. Nonetheless, Porete's work survived and circulated anonymously, gaining great popularity and influence. It was only in the mid-twentieth century that the much-loved text was identified as the condemned work (thereby casting considerable doubt on the original verdict against her).

Porete is extraordinarily bold: drawing particularly on the Song of Songs, she expresses the traditional themes of apophasis in the contemporary language of courtly love. The full title of her work is *The Mirror of the Simple Souls Who Are Annihilated and Remain Only in Will and Desire of Love*. 'Annihilation' is her word for the state of the soul in union with God; she also refers to it as liberated and perfected. Porete makes the *Mirror*'s purpose clear: not to describe the ascent to union but to take us to the place where grace may effect it. Her words must move us, and then get out of the way because words cannot do the work of grace. So McGinn describes this text as 'designed to implode – first back into the soul, and finally, when the soul is truly annihilated, back into the Divine Abyss'.[7]

As *The Mirror* traces the soul's journey towards union, all the 'self'-regarding content of the soul is annihilated: self-will,

self-awareness, selfish desire. Porete shares the apophatic teachers' insistence that popular piety, whether understood in terms of
conventional 'works' such as fasting, charity and asceticism, or the
more spiritual practices of prayer and devotion to the sacraments,
is deadly insofar as we seek through it to satisfy our own will, our
spiritual ambition. To be annihilated is to strip off all such ambition, to strip so consistently and radically that we become nothing,
no-thing. Divine unknowing, we saw earlier, is the opposite of stark
ignorance; it fails to catch knowledge because it is full to overflow-
ing with divine reality. In a similar way the soul is caught up in God
who is no-thing, and in union with the divine becomes 'nothinged'.
Paul Mommaers describes this as the emergence of 'An "I" without
a me'.[8] So, paradoxically, it is by being no-thing that we become one
with the One God, in a dynamic activity that excludes all duality.
The annihilated soul remains a soul, with nothing left to limit or
obstruct the free play of love, freed to be most fully itself, a human
person sharing the life of God.

Porete speaks of a union that grows and deepens: describing
the soul's ascent in seven stages, by the fifth she already finds that
'The Divine Goodness shows Himself to her [the soul] through the
goodness which draws her, transforms her and, through a joining
of goodness, unites her into pure Divine Goodness'; in the sixth,
the soul is 'freed, and pure and clarified from all things', so fully
one with God that no separate space remains, no ground for consciousness 'of' self or God, but only divine consciousness itself. Of
the highest stage she has nothing more to say than that we enter it
'in glory, of which none know how to speak'.[9]

The Mirror of Simple Souls treats its readers as living persons,
drawing them into conversation, into a dialogue between text and
reader and into an inner conversation where the different aspects of
the self urge one another to greater desire and greater understanding. The main speakers are 'Love', 'Reason' and 'the Soul', who speak
to one another in everyday language, not the technical jargon of
scholars. From time to time the sheer vitality of the soul's journey
into God overflows the constraints of conversational prose; Porete
breaks into song to declare and praise the union in which the Soul,
having no life independent of its loving Creator, becomes pregnant
with divinity:

Truth declares to my heart,
That I am loved by One alone,
And she says that it is without return
That He has given me His love.
This gift kills my thought
By the delight of His love,
Which delight
   lifts me and transforms me through union
Into the eternal joy
   of the being of divine Love.

And Divine Love tells me
   that she has entered within me,
And so she can do
   Whatever she wills,
Such strength she has given me,
From One Love whom I possess in love,
To whom I am betrothed,
Who wills what He loves,
And for this I will love Him.

I have said that I will love Him.
I lie, for I am not.
It is He alone who loves me:
He is, and I am not;
And nothing more is necessary to me
Than what He wills,
And that He is worthy.
He is fullness,
And by this am I impregnated.
This is the divine seed and Loyal Love.[10]

Notes

1 Maximus the Confessor, *Ambiguum 41* 1305 B–C, in Nicholas Constas' translation, *On Difficulties in the Church Fathers: The Ambigua*, Vol. 2 (Cambridge, MA: Harvard University Press, 2014), p. 105.

2 Ibid. 1308 B, p. 109.

3 St John of the Cross, cited in Kieran Kavanaugh, *John of the Cross: Doctor of Light and Love* (New York: Crossroad, 1999), pp. 132–3; italics and brackets original.

4 *The Cloud of Unknowing* 6, in Clifton Wolters' translation for the Penguin Classics edition (London: Penguin, 1961), p. 68.

5 Michael A. Sells, *Mystical Languages of Unsaying* (Chicago: University of Chicago Press, 1994), pp. 10, 217.

6 Bernard McGinn, *The Flowering of Mysticism: Men and Women in the New Mysticism (1200–1350)* (New York: Crossroad, 1998), p. 244. As McGinn shows, there are grounds for arguing that Porete's condemnation was as much to do with ecclesial politics as to do with doctrinal orthodoxy.

7 Ibid., p. 250.

8 Paul Mommaers, 'La transformation d'amour selon Marguerite Porete', cited in McGinn, ibid., p. 248.

9 *The Mirror of Simple Souls* 118; in Ellen L. Babinsky's translation for the Classics of Western Spirituality series (New York: Paulist Press, 1993), pp. 192–4.

10 Ibid. 122, p. 201.

PART 3

Pioneers of Apophatic Faith

Carole Bury 'Ode to Hope', pencil.

Gregory of Nyssa

To contemporary ears, words like 'philosophy' and 'theology' tend to sound abstract and academic. All too easily they conjure up images of fat jargon-filled textbooks, dusty classrooms and a system that values intellectual brilliance over practical know-how. If we wish to trace the historical development of the Christian apophatic tradition, we should be careful not to assume that its habitat lies in such a system.

Although there certainly were similar problems in the ancient world, the men and women who developed the negative way were interested in the practical questions of how to live, how to follow the path of Christ in a world that looked increasingly unlike first-century Galilee, how to lay hold of the kingdom of God, which Jesus taught was already within our grasp, within and among us. The early giants of the apophatic tradition were Christian leaders and spiritual guides: bishops and priests, monastics and followers of the desert traditions. Inevitably, we learn about them now by reading them; and because their work is culturally unfamiliar, it can sound academic. As we begin to focus on some of these theologians and their writing, it's worth pausing to remember that these are lovers of wisdom, not of information. They have stood on holy ground and their words pour from hearts of love. Their theology is not simply 'talking about God' but words derived from the Living Word; they have heard the words of God in Scripture and received the Word sacramentally in the Eucharist, and now those holy words flow through them to draw us too towards God.

Gregory of Nyssa is one of three fourth-century theologians collectively known as 'The Cappadocians' because their home was in Cappadocia in central Turkey. Gregory's elder brother, Basil, became Bishop of Caesarea; the family's friend, Gregory, became Bishop of Nazianzus; the younger Gregory became Bishop of Nyssa. Between them they had a decisive impact on the development of the Church, including our understanding of the Trinity and the role of the Holy Spirit, and the development of communal monastic life. Of the three, Gregory of Nyssa is the tenderest soul: his *Life of Moses* and his sermon-commentaries on the Song of Songs, especially, are a deep well of spiritual treasures. It's interesting to note that the wisdom on which Gregory draws was not simply the fruit of solitary religious experience but of a large and talkative family home, where the women as well as the men, and their frequent guests, argued, debated, prayed and ate together.

One of the major debates of Gregory's day revolved around the question of whether or how far God can be known. Everyone agreed that we could know things God has chosen to reveal to us – so we could know about God's intentions for us, expressed in the Law given to the Jews and in Jesus, the Word incarnate; we could know about God's actions in history, recorded in the Scriptures; and about God's plans for the future, expressed through the prophets. But a sharp distinction was drawn between God as he has shown himself to us and God as he is in himself: in the language of Gregory's day, this is a distinction between the divine 'energies' – we would say 'activities' – and the divine essence. So the key question was: Is God's essence, God's own being, knowable?

On the opposite side of the debate from Gregory, Eunomius argued that God is indeed knowable. Not only does God know himself but we can too: we are able to name or define God, as the 'uncreated one'.

Gregory, on the other hand, insisted that God is unknowable; no matter how high we climb, how much we discover, God will always be more than we can grasp. Thus Gregory comments on the Song:

> The Bride speaks: 'Upon my bed by night I sought him whom my soul loves ... but found him not. I called him, but he gave no answer.' How indeed could she reach with a name the one who is above every name?[1]

The beyondness of God is usually referred to in theological language as 'transcendence'. But there is a problem with transcendence if it is taken as the opposite of immanence: it seems to neglect the crucial fact of the Incarnation. To put it another way, it seems to put God out of reach – and while Gregory's God may not be simply 'within our grasp' (as if we were able to determine when and how to make contact), he does nevertheless touch us. The divine beyondness for Gregory is not so much a matter of transcendence versus immanence as of infinity.

So when Gregory picks up the language of stripping off, he sees that it will be a never-ending process. We won't simply have to lay aside a set of wrong habits or ideas and replace them with a correct set, but any and all of them, over and over again, because: 'Every concept which comes from some comprehensible image by an approximate understanding and by guessing at the divine nature constitutes an idol of God and does not proclaim God.'[2] It is Gregory who notices that the city watchmen appear to strip the Bride of a garment she has already taken off. He says:

> So it is with our ascent towards God: each stage that we reach always reveals something heavy weighing on the soul. Thus in comparison with her new found purity, that very stripping of her tunic now becomes a kind of garment which those who find her must once again remove.[3]

Gregory does more than any Christian theologian before him to sift out the significance of divine infinity. God is beyond time and space; God is not a being among others but the source of all being. God's goodness, creativity and love are endless because God has no end, no boundary, no limit. And if there is no boundary, we can't quite speak of a 'core' or 'essence' either. So rather than saying that God has an unknowable essence (and then facing the question of why an all-knowing God would not know his own essence), it is better to say that God's essence cannot be known because God isn't quite the sort of thing that has an essence. Rowan Williams explains:

> The substance of God is not to be touched or known; it is an abstraction and, in a sense, a fantasy; there is no core of the

divine being to be grasped as the 'essential' quality of God, only the divine works; God willing to relate to the world in love. These works or operations are equally inaccessible to conceptualizing, simply because they are known only by being experienced, by the character of a life lived out of them and in their strength.[4]

What word-pictures can we use to describe a lifelong journey into deeper relationship with a God who is unknowable? Gregory found no better theme than that of darkness. We have already seen that spiritual writers often used a threefold pattern to describe the soul's journey towards God and to envisage it as a progressive enlightenment, a journey into greater and greater clarity. Before Gregory they tended to use the language of contemplation to describe the third and final stage, where the soul meets God. But contemplation is too close to seeing and knowing, as far as Gregory is concerned. For him, enlightenment and contemplation, the prayerful relishing of all that we can discover of God, belong in the second stage of the journey. In terms of what happens in the third stage, Gregory turned to the biblical texts that speak of an encounter beyond vision and comprehension.[5]

In both Moses' Sinai encounter and the Bride's longing for her lover in the Song, Gregory finds texts that clearly convey his theme: God can't be captured, either intellectually or existentially. But that doesn't mean God is absent or beyond our reach; it just means that we get closer by touch than by sight, closer by yearning than by thinking. God is personal and meets us personally, which also of course implies that even in a true and generous meeting, not everything is disclosed – with persons, it never is. Darkness captures this particularly well – we sort of bump into God in the darkness, encountering only one edge of the divine:

> [The Bride] is encompassed by a divine night, during which her Spouse approaches, but does not reveal Himself. But how can that which is invisible reveal itself in the night? By the fact that He gives the soul some sense of His presence, even while He eludes her clear apprehension, concealed as He is by the invisibility of His nature.[6]

For Gregory, darkness is much more than a way of talking about not being able to see, understand or define God. Darkness isn't about absence: on Sinai and in the Song it is a place of encounter, a real experience of God unknown. In this way darkness paradoxically offers us a truer knowledge of God than light does – because in darkness we realize that we haven't grasped more than a fraction of the divine, whereas in light we are tempted to think we have seen all there is.

To speak about a God who is beyond all concepts, words and definitions we need a language that will unsay itself. Gregory achieves this, following scriptural precedent, by using the language of touch and physical senses, which *cannot* be taken literally when used of God, who is non-physical. He also achieves it by using paradoxes and contradictions. The darkness in which God finds and touches us is a numinous darkness: we feel as if we are in a 'watchful sleep' or as if we are 'soberly drunk'.[7]

Three wonderful consequences follow from Gregory's profound grasp of this truth, of the infinite and incomprehensible beyondness of God.

First, against the ghastly human tendency to suppose that we find God through the intellect, which makes learned people more likely than the less well-educated to know him well; which makes the ability to read the Bible in its original languages count for something in the holiness stakes; and which makes theological *in*formation an end in itself, rather than an aid to holy *trans*formation. Against all this, Gregory insists that God is not to be found by the intellect but by the heart, in love.

Second, although he is clear about the passive quality of holy encounter (that it is something that *happens to* us, not something we make happen), Gregory offers us a vision of a spiritual life that is active and practical. We remember his busy family home and also his elder brother Basil's growing monastic communities: Gregory is not thinking about an isolated spiritual life. Preaching on the Beatitudes, he pauses over Jesus' words, 'Blessed are the poor in spirit, for theirs is the kingdom of heaven.' To be blessed, he says, is to be like God. As is clear by now, being like God can't mean having an essence or nature similar to God's; nor can it mean knowing

God and thinking about the same things God thinks about. It can only mean sharing the 'energies' of God, behaving as God behaved in Jesus. In Jesus we discover what true poverty of spirit is: it is voluntary humility (Philippians 2.7 and Christ's self-emptying, again), expressed in action.[8] Similarly, preaching on the Lord's Prayer, Gregory says:

> To become like God means to become just, holy, and good and suchlike things. If anyone, as far as in him lies, clearly shows in himself the characteristics of these virtues, he will pass automatically and without effort from this earthly life to the life of Heaven.[9]

Here and in many other passages, Gregory is clear: if you seek to know God, your first and best route is to work out in practice what it means to live as love.

Third, since God is infinite, we can never exhaust God. However far we go in holy encounter there will be a vast beyond, the ever-newness of God. Although with the benefit of hindsight we might see this as almost obvious, it is something radically new, a gem mined in Gregory's exploration of the divine darkness. Earlier theologians saw the goal of the spiritual life as the terminus of a journey, a state of blessed rest in God. Gregory sees divinity as an open horizon, a never-ending adventure in love. The word that seems to sum this up for Gregory is *epektasis*, derived from the word Paul uses in Philippians 3.13–14, 'one thing I do, forgetting what lies behind and *straining forward* to what lies ahead, I press on . . .'. Gregory's genius was to place this 'straining forward' not simply on the road before the goal is reached but also on the road that plunges deeper into the heart of divinity. In the Song of Songs the lover does not only sing of searching for the beloved before they meet; she searches for him also after they have met.

Genesis tells us that humanity was created in the 'image and likeness' of God. Daringly, Gregory seems to be saying that the infinity and unknowability of God have an image in the human soul: we are made in relationship with God, and our desire for him is never exhausted; and because our desire is infinite we are in a sense never complete, never finished – there is always more of ourselves to be discovered in relationship with God. We continue to be created, for ever. The true self, 'hidden with Christ in God' (Colossians 3.3), turns out to have no fixed or final essence either, except this straining yearning pouring itself out towards the beloved. Unlike other desires, which can be sated, this desire grows by what it feeds on:

> But every desire for the Good which is attracted to that ascent constantly expands as one progresses in pressing on to the Good. This truly is the vision of God: never to be satisfied in the desire to see him. But one must always, by looking at what he can see, rekindle his desire to see more. Thus, no limit would interrupt growth in the ascent to God, since no limit to the Good can be found nor is the increasing of desire brought to an end because it is satisfied.[10]

Gregory's insistence on divine unknowability doesn't place God completely beyond our reach, then. It doesn't create an artificial and ultimately indefensible boundary between divine activity and divine nature, as if somehow God might be some kind of actor, behaving among us in ways that tell us nothing about divine character. It doesn't mean we can't say anything about God; it just means that God overflows everything we might ever say. We can't exhaust him, or ourselves, in the journey or the dance. It doesn't mean we can never arrive at our goal; it just means we'll never stop arriving.

Notes

1 *Homilies on the Song of Songs* 6, cited in Olivier Clément, *The Roots of Christian Mysticism* (London: New City, 1993), p. 27.

2 *Life of Moses*, translated by Abraham J. Malherbe and Everett Ferguson, in Classics of Western Spirituality series edition (New York: Paulist Press, 1978), p. 96.

3 *Commentary on the Song* XII, in Herbert Musurillo's translation of Jean Daniélou, *From Glory to Glory* (London: Murray, 1962), p. 264.

4 Rowan Williams, *The Wound of Love: Christian Spirituality from the New Testament to St John of the Cross* (London: Darton, Longman & Todd, 1979), p. 62.

5 Commenting on *Song of Songs* 5.2, Gregory says: 'Our initial withdrawal from wrong and erroneous ideas of God is a transition from darkness to light. Next comes a closer awareness of hidden things, and by this the soul is guided through sense phenomena to the world of the invisible. And this awareness is a kind of

cloud, which overshadows all appearances, and slowly guides and accustoms the soul to look towards what is hidden. Next the soul makes progress through all those stages and goes on higher, and as she leaves below all that human nature can attain, she enters within the secret chamber of divine knowledge, and here she is cut off on all sides by the divine darkness. Now she leaves outside all that can be grasped by sense or by reason, and the only thing left for her contemplation is the invisible and the incomprehensible. And here God is, as the Scriptures tell us . . . "*But Moses went to the dark cloud wherein God was*" (Exod. 20.21).' *Commentary on the Song* XI: 1001, translated in Daniélou, ibid., p. 247; italics original.

6 *Commentary on the Song* XI: 1001 B–C, translated in Daniélou, ibid., cited in Louth, *The Origins of the Christian Mystical Tradition* (Oxford: Clarendon Press, 1981), p. 94.

7 For example, see Sermon 10 on the Song of Songs.

8 Gregory's first *Sermon on the Beatitudes*; a translation by H. C. Graef is available in the Ancient Christian Writers series, Vol. 18 (New York: Paulist Press, 1954), pp. 89–91.

9 Sermon 2 on 'Our Father who art in Heaven', also translated by Graef, ibid., p. 42.

10 *Life of Moses* II.238–9, translated by Malherbe and Ferguson, ibid., p. 116.

The Dionysian Corpus

One of the most brilliant and shocking documents of the apophatic tradition is one of the shortest. Titled *The Mystical Theology*, it opens not by talking about God but by addressing God in prayer:

> Trinity!! Higher than any being,
>   any divinity, any goodness!
> Guide of Christians
>   in the wisdom of heaven!
> Lead us up beyond unknowing and light,
>   up to the farthest, highest peak
>   of mystic scripture,
>   where the mysteries of God's Word
>   lie simple, absolute and unchangeable
>   in the brilliant darkness of a hidden silence.
> Amid the deepest shadow
>   they pour overwhelming light
>   on what is most manifest.
>   Amid the wholly unsensed and unseen
>   they completely fill our sightless minds
>   with treasures beyond all beauty.[1]

In just a few lines we meet so many familiar apophatic themes: the mountain ascent, unknowing, the paradoxes of speaking silence, brilliant darkness and sightless seeing, the beyondness of God unmasking the inadequacy of even our most treasured language of divinity and goodness. All of it is contained in a prayer, indicating that this is not a philosophical or intellectual approach but a spiritual one; a path leading not away from faith but further towards holy encounter.

The Mystical Theology consists of five short chapters. In the first chapter this text is addressed like a letter of advice to 'Timothy, my friend', who seeks 'a sight of the mysterious things'. It tells him to 'strive upwards', 'abandoning' or 'shedding' not only 'all things' but himself also, and assures him of the goal: 'union with him who is beyond all being and knowledge'. There is a cautionary note: none of this will make sense, or be helpful, to people 'who think that by their own intellectual resources they can have a direct knowledge of him who has made the shadows his hiding place'. Timothy is a Greek name meaning 'God-fearer': whether or not there was ever a specific Timothy to whom this work was addressed, this advice is clearly applicable to anyone who fears God – for 'The fear of the LORD is the beginning of wisdom' (Psalm 111.10 and elsewhere).

If he is going to understand what follows, Timothy is told, he must understand the nature of this 'negative' theology:

> What has actually to be said about the Cause of everything is this. Since it is the Cause of all beings, we should posit and ascribe to it all the affirmations we make in regard to beings, and, more appropriately, we should negate all these affirmations, since it surpasses all being.[2]

In the second chapter we are reminded of the analogy explored earlier with classical sculptors, who chip away at stone to arrive at the image hidden within; the third chapter offers further explanation. The final two chapters are breathtakingly daring. It's hard to read them, even now, without feeling a sense of vertigo, that need to reach out for a handhold against the dizziness.

We are taken systematically through the process of ascent by negation. At its lowest reaches are 'privations' – concepts that are purely negative in form, denoting a complete lack of something. These are easily denied in relation to the divine Cause of all: it is 'not inexistent, lifeless, speechless, mindless'.[3] Then comes a long list, broken into two main categories, of things that might be positively said of the Creator, 'ascribing to it all the affirmations we make in regard to beings'. The lowest category concerns things we tend to say about the material world, characteristics we can learn by sense perception: that something has shape or weight, is visible or tangible, changes, moves and so on. This category is the source of many rich images and metaphors for God in the Bible and Christian tradition, but it doesn't tend to cost us much to admit that they aren't actually (literally) *true*. So these are all denied. The higher category – at this point we are beginning the final chapter of *The Mystical Theology* – concerns immaterial reality, the kind of things known by the mind rather than the senses. It includes things like beauty and truth, power, wisdom, goodness and relationship. Denying these feels brutal, but Timothy is given no reprieve:

> [The Cause of everything] has no power, it is not power, nor is it light. It does not live nor is it life. It is not a substance, nor is it eternity or time. It cannot be grasped by the understanding since it is neither knowledge nor truth. It is not kingship. It is not wisdom. It is neither one nor oneness, divinity nor good-ness . . .[4]

So far we have negated or denied first privations and then affir-mations, rising from things that are rarely or only peripherally said about God the Creator, to affirmations that sit at the heart of Scripture and devotion. At the final stage of the ascent the nega-tions also must be negated, for God 'is both beyond every assertion, being the perfect and unique cause of all things, and, by virtue of its pre-eminently simple and absolute nature, free of every limitation, beyond every limitation; it is also beyond every denial'.[5] No words are left. Every kind of talk about God has been stripped away. Every mental or spiritual state that might have been nourished by such talk has been laid aside. The text ends in silence. If the words of the opening prayer will be answered, it is God himself who has led Timothy thus far and who awaits him in the silence.

Throughout *The Mystical Theology* it is clear that this process of negation is not a flat-out assault on religious language. The object is not to devastate the terrain; it is a steady, graded ascent:

> Is it not closer to reality to say that God is life and goodness rather than that he is air or stone? Is it not more accurate to deny that drunkenness and rage can be attributed to him than to deny that we can apply to him the terms of speech and thought?[6]

A careful reader will note, however, that 'air', 'stone', 'drunkenness' and 'rage' actually are words used of God, metaphorically, in Scripture and tradition. This leads us on to one of the most extraordinary insights of this writer, the idea of the 'unlike likenesses' of God, explored in a text called *The Celestial Hierarchy*, again addressed to Timothy.

Timothy is reminded of the many metaphors and images in the Bible, including 'flaming wheels whirling in the skies . . . material thrones . . . multicolored horses . . . [and] spear-carrying lieutenants'; these are evidence of the wisdom of Scripture, which uses them 'as a concession to the nature of our own mind'.[7] The images 'uplift our mind in a manner suitable to our nature'. In other words, if we are at a stage on the journey where it will be helpful to contemplate God through the great prophetic visions of Ezekiel (1.15–21) and Daniel (7.9), with their 'wheels in the skies', these images are to be used and affirmed. But once we have digested them, we need to pass on, not allowing them to limit our search, becoming – as Gregory would say – a kind of idol for us to cling to, but putting them aside so that we can ascend higher. Clearly, 'life' and 'goodness' will indeed lift our minds higher towards God than 'air' and 'stone'.

However, *The Celestial Hierarchy* boldly suggests that there is an important sense in which the lowest, most basic images are 'much more appropriate' than the higher ones.[8] They are more suitable images for God, precisely because they lay bare the mechanics of theological speech; because they are much more resistant to becoming idols; because they push us in the direction of negation. The higher up the ascent we go, the less obvious it is that we will have to eat our words. How true this is! Christians sing Brian Doerksen's song 'Faithful One', which includes the line 'You are my rock in times of trouble' (Psalm 18.2; 2 Samuel 22.3), and are most unlikely to think that their God really is made of stone. Many more will sing Jarrod Cooper's 'King of Kings, Majesty' without the same kind of critical distance from the words. Yet the tendency to identify God too closely with kingship has inarguably done a great deal more damage among God's people than the tendency to identify him with stone. The rock, in that sense, is simply a better image: less harmful, more effective in getting us to see the wisdom in it at the same time as the wisdom beyond it.

We have admitted so far that the unlike likenesses, the images of God as wheels of fire or rock and so on, belong in the foothills of the divine ascent. They are basic, and precisely because they're basic they're sometimes the best images to use. But *The Celestial Hierarchy* has one last shock for us: in a sense, they're no better and no worse than the 'higher' images, the ones that seem a lot more similar to God. To understand why, we need to return to Gregory and his understanding of the infinity of God. If the summit of the ascent is infinitely far away – if it is, in a sense, without a terminus – then the foothills are not further from it and the higher pastures are not nearer: 'for the Deity is far beyond every manifestation of being and of life; no reference to light can characterize it; every reason or intelligence falls short of similarity to it.'[9] Thus radical negation and the deliberate use of unlike likenesses will characterize our apophatic speech, if we are willing to learn from Timothy's teacher. One more major new theme comes from this source: the language of unknowing. Inadequate words – all words, that is – are not only to be unsaid but unlearned, unknown.

We have, in addition to the dogmatic texts, ten letters ascribed to this author (none addressed to Timothy, though he is referred to in Letter 9). In the first of them the practice of unknowing is explained. We are not to think of the kind of ignorance that just refers to a lack or deprivation of knowledge; that is like the kind of darkness that can be dispelled by light. Just as there is a higher darkness at the top of Sinai, a pregnant and shining darkness, so there is another kind of ignorance, a holy unknowing that transcends our knowing of all that is knowable: 'And this quite positively complete unknowing is knowledge of him who is above everything that is known.'[10] Whereas negation or unsaying is a process, a continual practice along the whole of the ascent (or, in the more passive language these texts prefer, the process of being 'lifted up'), unknowing not only describes the repeated decision 'not to know' ideas along the way but also, and more often, a state of being, the mental state of one who has come into the cloud atop Sinai. If God is beyond knowledge, then unknowing is the state of mind in which we meet him. According to the fifth letter:

> it is here that is found everyone worthy to know God and to look upon him. And such a one, precisely because he neither sees him

nor knows him, truly arrives at that which is beyond all seeing and all knowledge. Knowing exactly this, that he is beyond everything perceived and conceived, he cries out with the prophet, 'Knowledge of you is too wonderful for me; it is high, I cannot attain it'. (Psalm 139.6)[11]

So unknowing is different from ignorance, both in that it knows it cannot know and also in that it has gone beyond knowledge, has digested the wisdom of knowledge about God's activities all the way up to their highest point, and has kept itself free of entanglement in concepts. In the state of holy unknowing, the mind is not a blank: it is full of wonder and glory.

Apophatic spirituality turns out to be as exhausting – as well as exhilarating – as mountaineering. There is no excuse here for avoiding some of the hard work of biblical study and theology. We can't just say, 'Well, no need to study this because in the end we'll have to deny it', any more than we can get to the summit without going up the mountain. As we've already noticed, apophasis isn't opposed to or competing against kataphasis; kataphasis *gives* us the mountain we need to climb.

These apophatic texts are riven with paradox. We can hope to arrive where the God who is beyond everything will be present to us. There is an ascent to God through negation, although in another sense no words or ideas will get us closer than any others. The ascent takes us up through narrower and narrower ways until it ends in silence, where all words have failed; and yet it is marked also by an explosion of linguistic creativity, leading to virtually untranslatable tongue-twisters where words are vertiginously piled up in a manner reminiscent of the Song of Songs: towards the beginning of a treatise on *The Divine Names*, God is described as 'the divinely sovereign beyond-beingness, which is the beyond-existence of the beyond-goodness'.[12]

∗∗∗

The small collection of texts we call the 'Dionysian corpus' has had an almost immeasurable influence on the development of Christian spiritual thought.[13] Up to this point, though, we haven't said anything about who wrote them.

In the early years of the sixth century after Christ, somewhere in Syria – probably – someone composed this set of diamantine texts containing the Christian tradition's most startling account of apophasis. They were promulgated under a pseudonym: the name Dionysius the Areopagite is that of St Paul's first-century Athenian convert, mentioned in Acts 17.34 (hence the writer is sometimes referred to as 'Pseudo-Dionysius').[14] No one has convincingly established who the author really was, or the motivation for the pseudonym. We should note, though, that the use of a pseudonym isn't to be taken as indicating a sort of fraud: in the ancient world it could simply be a respectful way of indicating that one's work comes out of a particular tradition, so the wisdom in it is not exactly the author's own but belongs to the great teachers of the tradition.

Whatever its exact motivation, the use of a pseudonym is highly significant. By refraining from identifying the real author, the texts perform a sort of stripping off, a denial of self; in their relentless focus away from a particular context and towards divine reality, they rehearse John the Baptist's 'He must increase, but I must decrease' (John 3.30). Even more importantly, they implicitly point towards one of the great gifts of apophatic spirituality, namely its capacity to defuse doctrinal divisions. At the time these texts appear to have arisen, the Christian Church was deeply and painfully divided by debates about the nature of Christ, about exactly how one living being might possibly have been both fully divine and fully human. These disagreements were not confined to some gentle world of theological scholarship: for two or more centuries already, bishops had been deposed and exiled, priests excommunicated, books and buildings burnt, anathemas proclaimed over differences in words and ideas. The Dionysian corpus was first quoted in circles associated with Monophysitism, a theological approach to the nature of Christ that was rejected as 'heretical' by the majority of churches. This may indicate that the author himself – assuming it was a 'he' – came from such circles. Or it may simply indicate that they knew the work and saw its implications. Either way, the one who took Dionysius' name was clear that *everything* we say about the divine contains some truth to feed someone at a particular stage on the path, and *nothing* we say about the divine will stand for long without negation. The figure of Dionysius the Areopagite in Acts 17 is one who brings together by his conversion two worlds of thought that some saw as utterly opposed, 'Athens' versus 'Jerusalem' or, in Paul's words, the wisdom of the world and the wisdom of God. In Letter 7, Dionysius says:

> In my view, good men are satisfied to know and to proclaim as well as they can the truth itself as it really is . . . It is therefore superfluous for someone expounding the truth to enter into dispute with this one or that, for each one says that his own bit of money is the real thing when in fact what he says may be a counterfeit copy of some part of the truth.[15]

Thus apophasis validates theological debate: different views can be seen as complementary 'parts of the truth' rather than as competing accounts of all truth. At the same time, apophasis defuses theological dispute and offers a space for reconciliation: ultimately, nobody knows!

Notes

1 *The Mystical Theology* I.1; here and for subsequent references to the works of Pseudo-Dionysius I refer to Colm Luibheid's translation in the Classics of Western Spirituality series, *Pseudo-Dionysius: The Complete Works* (London: SPCK, 1987).

2 Ibid., p. 136.

3 Ibid., p. 140.

4 Ibid., p. 141.

5 Ibid.

6 Ibid., p. 140.

7 *The Celestial Hierarchy*, ibid., pp. 147–8.

8 Ibid., p. 150.

9 Ibid., p. 149.

10 Ibid., p. 263.

11 Ibid., p. 265.

12 My translation of *The Divine Names* 593C. Luibheid marginally softens the impact in his translation: 'the supra-essential being of God – transcendent goodness transcendently there'; ibid., p. 54.

13 Brief and helpful chapters on the influence of the Dionysian corpus by Jaroslav Pelikan, Jean Leclercq and Karlfried Froehlich are included in the Classics of Western Spirituality volume.

14 Dionysius the Areopagite was traditionally identified with the bishop and martyr of Paris, Saint Denis; hence the author of these works is also sometimes referred to in English as Denis or Denys.

15 In Luibheid's translation, p. 266.

Meister Eckhart

As children many of us played 'ring-a-ring o' roses': linking hands in a circle, we sang while whirling around as fast as we could, until collapsing at the end in a panting, giggling heap. We were blithely oblivious to the words' resonances with tragic deaths by plague; to us it was just exhilarating and joyous play. If theologies had soundtracks, then ring-a-ring o' roses might well be the soundtrack to the work of Meister Eckhart. A late thirteenth-/early fourteenth-century scholar, preacher, religious administrator and spiritual guide, Eckhart's teachings whirl so fast that their meaning is hard to catch; you have to allow yourself to be swept along. The pace may at times make you anxious and giddy, but the music is always joyous.

The Song of Songs is never far away from Eckhart's thought; as well as writing a commentary on it, he refers to it frequently in his sermons and treatises. There is a part of us, he says, our innermost being – he calls it by many names, such as 'spark', 'little castle', 'the soul's power', 'the soul's height' – that is always orientated towards God, as the face of a flower turns towards the sun. The whole text of the Song, he declares, is about the 'mutual glance between God and the height of the soul', and this mutual glance is 'full of truth and delight'. Eckhart cites Song 5.6, 'My soul melted when my beloved spoke'; and like the Song's lover, he turns to natural images to express this delight:

> I have often said that there is a power in the soul that touches neither time nor flesh. It flows from the spirit and remains in the spirit, and is wholly spiritual. In this power God is always verdant and blossoming in all the joy and the honour that he is in himself. That is a joy so heartfelt, a joy so incomprehensible and great that no-one can tell it all.[1]

Our delight in God overflows; we rejoice in all that God orders and creates. There is joy in being what we were made to be: this is God's good gift to us, and in a sense just by being ourselves we glorify him.[2] This includes the pleasures of bodily existence, especially of the senses so important to the Song: taste and touch.[3] We give as well as receive joy, in a reciprocal flow: in honouring and serving God, Eckhart says, we give joy to the saints and angels, and 'God himself takes such delight in this, just as if it were his blessedness.'[4]

St Paul's apophatic insight, that 'It is no longer I who live, but Christ who lives in me' (Galatians 2.20), is clearly visible between the lines of much of Eckhart's teaching. Characteristically, this sense of the life of Christ within the soul is a source of joy. Eckhart also seizes on Paul's image of childbirth: any pain and suffering as we undergo the birth of Christ in us will later be forgotten in 'full and perfect delight'.[5]

In his German-language sermons in particular there are moments when the text seems to reveal not just what Eckhart said to his audience but how he said it; we sense his delight in this audience and his humble awareness of their delight in him. Preaching on the Annunciation, for example, Eckhart is moved to the verge of tears:

What God gives is his being, and his being is his goodness, and his goodness is his love. All sorrow and joy come from love. On the way, when I had to come here, I was thinking that I did not want to come here because I would become wet with tears of love. If you have ever been wet with tears of love . . .

We imagine a pause and the looks exchanged between preacher and audience as he struggles against a wobbling voice, looks of mutual recognition, palpable trust and spiritual intimacy, before he collects himself and continues: '. . . let us leave that aside for now.'[6]

The Song of Songs may speak of desolation and loss but it is always within the context of a love given and received, in mutual delight and joy. It is because of the joy already experienced, and the desire for more, that the lover goes out, braves the watchmen and seeks her beloved. This is Eckhart's theme: whatever the complexity, arduousness and apparent 'negativity' of the apophatic way, its motive force and sustaining power is holy joy. He cites the words Richard of St Victor gives to the soul:

What is that sweetness that is accustomed to touch me from time to time and affects me so strongly and deliciously that I begin in a way to be completely taken out of myself, and to be carried away I know not where? All at once I am renewed and entirely changed; I begin to feel well in a way that lies beyond description. Consciousness is lifted on high, and all the misery of past misfortunes is forgotten. The intellectual soul rejoices; the understanding is strengthened, the heart is enlightened, the desires satisfied. I already see myself in a different place that I do not know. I hold something within in love's embrace, but I do not know what it is.[7]

Eckhart is exuberant and bold; his whirling theological dance does not make for careful steps. He has little time for studied religiosity. The bold apophatic statements that are set out in such a careful and orderly structure by Dionysius are let off like firecrackers in Eckhart's sermons and discourses: the heart that is close to God, he says, is free from prayer; asking God for things is treating him as a servant, not as God. Similarly, you shouldn't love God – that's cupboard love; or better, you should love him 'as a non-God'. Contradicting St Paul, love is not the greatest virtue: detachment is. God needs us: he can't be God without us. We are greater than God; we can compel him to work in us; and we are nothing.

Unsurprisingly, the religious authorities were deeply uneasy. Despite Eckhart's popularity and brilliant reputation, his teaching was twice examined by inquisitors, first locally in Cologne and then in the papal capital at Avignon. Eckhart died shortly before the verdict of heresy was pronounced against a list of 26 points drawn from his teaching (15 were judged to contain heresy and a further 11 to be 'rash and suspect of heresy'). He insisted that he was never a heretic; modern scholars, noting – just as he argued – how well-rooted his ideas are in the Church's traditional teachings, including those of Augustine, Dionysius and Thomas Aquinas, have tended to agree.

You don't understand the 'meaning' of a game unless you join in. Similarly, participation is key to Eckhart's approach to teaching: you have to put yourself at risk, to 'have skin in the game', as we say nowadays, if you want to learn. He tells the story of St Antony struggling with tormenting spirits, in a clear echo of Jacob's wrestling-match at Jabbok Ford:

> When he had overcome his distress, our Lord appeared joyfully to him in bodily form. Then the holy man said, 'O dear Lord, wherever were you when I was in such need?' Then our Lord said, 'I was here, just where I am now; but it was my will and my pleasure to see how valiant you might be.'[8]

So, Eckhart explains, when we read the Bible we need to look 'under the shell of the letter', to mine it for the 'more hidden sense'. Again, the discovery of meaning through this process is a source of delight: 'it is like bringing honey forth from the hidden depths of the honeycomb.'[9] In his own work just as in Scripture, paradox, pun, striking imagery and unusual wordplay all force the reader to wrestle, and make impossible any fixed or stable reading of his meaning.

From time to time in his more speculative works, Eckhart pauses to remind us that those at different stages on the journey will find different truths appropriate and helpful. His method is 'multiple exposition', offering a range of ideas 'so that the reader can freely take now one and now the other as seems useful to him'.[10] Often those meanings appear as flat contradictions: God is everything and nothing, known and unknown, God and not-God. The shift between these levels of meaning can be carefully signposted: Eckhart sometimes introduces each new step with 'I say more . . .'.

He reflects at one point on the scholarly exclusivity that restricts higher teaching to an inner circle of experts; by contrast, his teaching is open to all, despite the risk of misunderstanding, because the inexpert need to be able to learn, just as the sick are the ones who need a doctor. In any case, it is only by God's grace that the teacher's words will enable us to 'find the truth within ourselves'.[11] Eckhart insists that there is no exclusivity in detachment or joy:

But I say yet more (do not be afraid for this joy is close to you and is in you): there is not one of you who is so cross-grained, so feeble in understanding or so remote but he may find this joy within himself, in truth, as it is, with joy and understanding, before you leave this church today, indeed before I have finished preaching . . .[12]

In an extraordinary sermon on Matthew 5.3, 'Blessed are the poor', he once again offers different layers of teaching ('I have often said . . . but now I say . . .'), before concluding in pastoral mercy: 'Whoever does not understand what I have said, let him not burden his heart with it.'[13]

If we all see the truth differently according to where we stand, and according to who and how we are, then how will we know when and in what direction to move from our current viewpoint? Eckhart's answer is simple: follow where the joy leads. And that direction is the one laid down for us in Exodus and the Song of Songs: we move towards nakedness, which Eckhart links up with a host of associated images – emptiness, virginity, detachment, humility, poverty, wilderness, being and becoming nothing, and 'living without a why'.

Nakedness means casting off all attachments. Most obviously that means ceasing to be attached to created things, but Eckhart isn't proposing a world-hating spirituality, as is clear from his delight in creation. Instead his logic is built on the apophatic insistence that God is beyond all creatures, not as a greater sort of being but as no-being at all. Creatures are limited, boundaried, defined; God is not. The only definition that can be offered for the God whose name is no-name is that he is beyond definition. Therefore it isn't a question of our attaching to God instead of to creatures. To paraphrase Augustine, if you can attach to it, it isn't God. It's no surprise, then, that Eckhart echoes Gregory of Nyssa's insistence that the journey deeper into God will never end, never let us put down roots: 'The more you have of God, the more you long for him, for if you could be content with God, and such a contentment with him were to come, God would not be God.'[14] Eckhart sees attachment as rooted in possessiveness, and in order to be able to possess something, we have to be able to 'comprehend' it, to get our minds or hands around it. Like the monkey in the fable whose hand is trapped in the cookie-jar because of what is in its closed fist, we can only be free if we will stop holding on. Again, we can only love the world as it is if we stop holding on. Denys Turner explains Eckhart's logic of detachment:

> the undetached person denatures her world and cannot even properly enjoy it. She cannot meet with reality on its own terms, but only on her own. Detachment, for Eckhart, is not the severing of desire's relation with its object, but the restoration of desire to a proper relation of objectivity; as we might say, of reverence for its object. Detachment is therefore the basis of the true possibility of love, which is why, for Eckhart, it is more fundamental than love, being the condition of its possibility.[15]

Once we let go of created things and find God, the Creator, then we will regain all things in him, but without possession, for 'God shines in all things.'[16]

What we are most inclined to cling to, though, isn't 'creatures' in general but what we hold most dear: the self, our image of God and the spiritual comforts that assure us of his presence. Eckhart has sharp words for people who cling to 'good works', to moral, spiritual and religious practices: 'Every attachment to every work deprives one of the freedom to wait upon God.'[17] As an experienced spiritual director, he knows that such works feed our sense of self, even while we tell ourselves we do them for God: 'Your heart, your intellect, your body, your soul, your powers, everything about you and in you, all of it is sick and spoiled. So take refuge in him . . .'[18] So we need to 'go outside' of ourselves, strip off the self, put a stop to all self-love and self-regard. There Eckhart is on firmly biblical ground: we are to deny ourselves, to decrease so that Christ may increase.

With beautiful simplicity Eckhart reasons that if we withdraw fully from all that is limited there will be no place left for us to stand except in God. This is ecstasy in its most literal sense: Eckhart has no time for esoteric and unusual mystical experiences; ecstasy isn't an otherworldly rapture, just 'standing outside' (*ek-stasis*) oneself, and the glory of it is that God joins us when we do it: 'O my dear man, what harm does it do you to allow God to be God in you? Go completely out of yourself for God's love, and God comes completely out of himself for love of you.'[19] Just as in the Song of Songs' bold imagery, therefore, it is not only the lover but also the beloved who must become naked. Eckhart laments the way our religiosity tends to do the opposite, swathing God in extra layers. In the end this is not the devotion it appears, rather it is a way of taking the risk out of divine encounter, domesticating it and making it safe:

> truly, when people think that they are acquiring more of God in inwardness, in devotion, in sweetness and in various approaches than they do by the fireside or in the stable, you are acting just as if you took God and muffled his head up in a cloak and pushed him under a bench.[20]

Still, our capacity for self-delusion goes very deep. Eckhart insists that stripping naked applies not just to our love, will and attachments but most of all to the mind. Just as quite a small piece of paper stuck to a window can block out the whole sun from our sight, so any mental image or idea of God, Eckhart says, can be 'as great as God is great. Why? Because it comes between you and the whole of God.'[21] When we pray and ask God for something, we paper over the unnameable with a named God – Saviour, Father, Creator. When we do something 'for' God, the same happens. Whenever we enter into any sort of transaction with the divine, we are imagining a God who is defined by a particular kind of relation to us – a defined image; another word for that, of course, is 'idol'. So Eckhart concludes his sermon on Ephesians 4.23 ('be renewed in your spirit'):

> Therefore your soul must be unspiritual, free of all spirit, and must remain spiritless; for if you love God as he is God, as he is spirit, as he is person and as he is image – all this must go! 'Then how should I love him?' You should love him as he is a non-God, a nonspirit, a nonperson, a nonimage, but as he is a pure, unmixed, bright 'One', separated from all duality; and in

that One we should eternally sink down, out of 'something' into 'nothing'.

May God help us to that. Amen.[22]

At the end of the ascent through negations performed in Dionysius' *Mystical Theology*, negation itself is negated and language is exhausted; silence prevails. Eckhart is driven by the same logic. If God is not limited in any way, then he cannot be simply 'beyond' all limited beings, as if they occupied a certain amount of space and the divinity had all the rest. That would still be a kind of limit (and it is why, in the end, love of God is not in competition with love of creatures). In terms of the distinction between transcendence (God beyond all) and immanence (God within all), God's true transcendence transcends transcendence: he is beyond the distinction, not limited to immanence, not limited to transcendence. Eckhart's older contemporary Marguerite Porete captured this exactly when she made 'FarNear' a designation for God.

So God is both far and near, in and beyond, known and unknown, named and above all names. Here again Eckhart can only speak of God either from one perspective or the other, which is why he often seems to contradict himself. When he wishes to draw our attention to the God who is 'hidden' behind our images of him, to point to the 'silent darkness of the hidden Fatherhood', Eckhart speaks at times of the 'Godhead beyond God', the 'ground' where God, like the soul, is naked, a pure 'nothing'. To approach this God we must enter the wilderness and wander there just as the saints of old. There is nothing there to guide us, feed us, shelter or support us. No path from 'here' to 'there', no 'before' filled with memories or 'after' envisioned by imagination, no 'why'. Stripped of all our resources we are no longer able to encounter God as one who 'is' or 'does'. If by grace divine encounter occurs, there is no 'self' or 'other', just the event of union. Thus for Eckhart, union has two faces: in one it is the lovers' encounter of the Song; in the other, all duality disappears,

then I must just become him, and he must become me. I say more: God must just become me, and I must just become God, so completely one that this 'he' and this 'I' become and are one 'is', and in this is-ness, eternally perform one work.[23]

In one sense this indistinct union beyond all knowing is the soul's beginning and end. As we said earlier, silence reigns. There is only joy.

In another sense, as the reference to the 'one work' of the united soul implies, the game continues. The God who is not a thing or a being continues to pour forth into all things and all beings, in and through and with us, unconstrained by us, 'for this "he", who is God, and this "I", which is the soul, are greatly fruitful.'[24] Centuries earlier Gregory of Nyssa had seen that, to repeat how Rowan Williams puts it:

> The substance of God is not to be touched or known; it is an abstraction and, in a sense, a fantasy; there is no core of the divine being to be grasped as the 'essential' quality of God, only the divine works, God willing to relate to the world in love.[25]

Eckhart is thoroughly faithful to this apophatic heritage. Having brought the soul into the wilderness he draws us back into the world to do God's work of love. By means of some outrageously creative wordplay he reinterprets the Gospel contrast between busy Martha and contemplative Mary, upending Jesus' teaching that Mary had 'the better part' (Luke 10.38–42). Martha is our model; she is presented – recalling Jesus' mother – as both 'virgin' and 'wife'. She is virgin in that she is detached, empty, naked, free; and if we wish to conceive Christ we must be such virgins, he insists. However:

> 'Wife' is the noblest word one can apply to the soul, much nobler than 'virgin'. That a man conceives God in himself is good, and in his conceiving he is a maiden. But that God should become fruitful in him is better . . . and then the spirit is a wife . . . when he for God gives birth again to Jesus in the heart of the Father.[26]

To give birth to Jesus in the heart of the Father is to be drawn fully and completely into the life of the Trinity, to be in God beyond self and world, and to overflow with God into incarnate life, into the work of Christ in the world, the creative and healing work of joy and love.

Notes

1 From Eckhart's sermon on Luke 10.38, *Intravit Jesus . . .*; in Edmund Colledge and Bernard McGinn's translation for the Classics of Western Spirituality series edition, *Meister Eckhart: The Essential Sermons, Commentaries, Treatises and Defense* (New York: Paulist Press, 1981), p. 179.

2 Sections 160–1 of the *Book of the Parables of Genesis*, ibid., p. 120.

3 Ibid. sections 155–6, pp. 117–8.

4 Sermon on Wisdom 5.16, *Iusti vivent*, ibid., p. 185.

5 *Commentary on John*, section 130, on verse 1.14, ibid., pp. 172–3.

6 Sermon *Ave, gratia plena*, ibid., p. 195.

7 *Commentary on John*, section 49, ibid., p. 139.

8 *The Book of Divine Consolation*, ibid., pp. 231–2.

9 Prologue to the *Book of the Parables of Genesis*, ibid., p. 93.

10 *Commentary on John*, section 39, ibid., p. 135.

11 *The Book of Divine Consolation*, ibid., p. 239.

12 From Sermon 66, cited in Bernard McGinn, *The Flowering of Mysticism* (New York: Crossroad, 1998), p. 14.

13 *The Book of Divine Consolation*, Colledge and McGinn, ibid., p. 203.

14 *Renovamini spiritu*, ibid., pp. 207–8.

15 Denys Turner, *The Darkness of God: Negativity in Christian Mysticism* (Cambridge: Cambridge University Press, 1995), p. 183.

16 *Counsels on Discernment* 6, Colledge and McGinn, ibid., p. 253.

17 *Intravit Jesus . . .*, ibid., p. 178.

18 *Counsels on Discernment* 16, ibid., p. 266.

19 Sermon on 1 John. 4.9, *In Hoc Apparuit*, ibid., p. 184.

20 Ibid., p. 182.

21 Ibid., p. 184.

22 *Renovamini spiritu*, ibid., p. 208.

23 Ibid.

24 Ibid.

25 Rowan Williams, *The Wound of Love: Christian Spirituality from the New Testament to St John of the Cross* (London: Darton, Longman & Todd, 1979), p. 62.

26 *Intravit Jesus . . .*, Colledge and McGinn, ibid., p. 178.

Nicholas of Cusa

'I see you prostrated most devoutly and weeping tears of love, not false tears but from the heart. Tell me who you are.'

'I am a Christian.'

'What are you worshipping?'

'God.'

'Who is the God you worship?'

'I do not know.'

'How can you so earnestly worship that which you do not know?'

'It is because I do not know that I worship.'[1]

After the giddiness and dancing complexity of Eckhartian apophasis, roughly a century and a half later the Italian scholar, diplomat, priest, cardinal and bishop, Nicholas of Cusa, robustly calls a spade not-a-spade. A true 'Renaissance man', Nicholas' writings cover theology, philosophy, canon law and ecclesiology, and draw on theory of art and geometry as much as on biblical and traditional wisdom; an open mind and a breadth of interest lead him to some astonishing anticipations of much later thought in cosmology, philosophy and politics, as well as to appreciation for the insights of cultures beyond the Catholic Church. Arguably it is his firm grasp of the truth of not-knowing that enables Nicholas to speculate to such powerful effect.

Nicholas' apophatic manifesto is *On Learned Ignorance*, published in 1440. In a letter to Cardinal Julian Cesarini, to whom the work is dedicated, he attributes his breakthrough insight not to scholarly study or persuasion but to a sudden experience of grace – a 'celestial gift from the Father of Lights'[2] – during a sea-voyage.

Under a vast and open sky Nicholas was digesting the experience of encounter with a Christianity that was the same but different: he had been in Constantinople, meeting theologians of the East, encountering icons and ancient texts. 'I was led' he says, by this experience, 'to embrace incomprehensibles incomprehensibly in learned ignorance'.

Nicholas expounds 'learned ignorance', 'instructed ignorance', 'sacred ignorance' as both a state of mind and a method. Whereas in some versions of apophasis our ignorance of the divine beyond is contrasted with our knowledge of the world, or in others our incapacity to know the transcendent God with the knowledge revealed in Christ the incarnate Son, Nicholas is thoroughgoing: we are ignorant concerning God *and* the world *and* Christ. His starting point is reminiscent of Gregory of Nyssa: we are to explore the implications of divine infinity. Knowledge requires boundaries to things that are to be named and measured, whose relations and distinctions it explores. Knowledge simply has no purchase on borderless infinity. For Nicholas, the divine infinity is 'absolute maximum'; the universe, as its created image, is also infinite, a 'contracted maximum'. He puts it another way: the universe is 'enfolded' in God; it is 'unfolded' in creation. Moreover, turning to divine unity: this isn't the kind of 'one' that can be counted, that is different from 'two' or more: it 'cannot be number . . . cannot be multiplied . . . cannot become number . . . Thus, deity is infinite unity.'[3]

Learned ignorance becomes a space for exploration, a school. In Book 1 of *On Learned Ignorance*, having explored the geometry of the infinite line, infinite circle and infinite triangle by means of the ancient technique of *aphairesis* (stripping away), Nicholas concludes that:

These considerations can assist the intellect . . . [which] can in sacred ignorance move greatly forward, above all understanding . . . For here we have now seen clearly how we arrive at God by removing the participation of beings . . . It is only in learned ignorance that we behold such being, for when I mentally remove all the things that participate being, nothing seems to remain. For this reason the great Dionysius says that an understanding of God approaches nothing rather than something. But sacred ignorance teaches me that what seems nothing to the intellect is the incomprehensible maximum.[4]

We are able, Nicholas avers, to become 'instructed in ignorance'.[5] By understanding these geometrical shapes, he says, 'from this knowledge we shall, in learned ignorance, attain to the Trinity';[6] we will learn 'that God is ineffable';[7] that only the 'absolute maximum' is self-originating and that everything else comes from it, and from this 'many things can become clear to us about the world or universe'.[8]

The ideas entertained in ignorance, 'above all understanding',[9] are epistemically modest. We see how little we know. We realize that our ideas are approximations at best – signs and images of what is beyond. Nicholas understands that imagination is of more help to us here than reason: 'If therefore . . . you wish truly to understand something about the motion of the universe, you must make use of your imagination as much as possible.'[10] Our investigations in ignorance, extending to ideas about Jesus, are able to 'increase our faith and perfection'.[11] Just as Paul asserts that knowledge comes to an end, but love never ends (1 Corinthians 13.8), so Nicholas finds that when there is no knowledge to hold on to, 'we can only marvel' at the works of God.[12] He concludes his exposition of sacred ignorance with a meditation on divine feasts that suggests both the lover's banqueting house of the Song of Songs, and the liturgy of the Eucharist – in words that surely also recall his own experience under the Adriatic stars:

> If in your mind you will meditate on these profound things, and indeed they are profound, a wonderful sweetness of spirit will engulf you. For by an inner savor you will detect, as with the most fragrant incense, the inexpressible goodness of God . . . You will be filled . . . without surfeit, for this immortal food is life itself . . . And . . . the blessed are forever drinking and are forever filled, but never have they drunk or been filled. Blessed be God . . .
>
> To this glory we triumphantly aspire with great affection and beseech God the Father, with suppliant hearts, that by God's Son, our Lord Jesus Christ, and in him by the Holy Spirit, God would,

out of God's immense mercifulness, grant us this glory in order that we may eternally enjoy God who is blessed forever.[13]

Among the 'many things' that learned ignorance makes clear about the universe are two characteristics of all finite things: first, that 'the identity of the universe exists in diversity'; second, that 'all are in all and each is in each'.[14] Against the grain of centuries-old traditions, Nicholas eschews any inference from holy simplicity to worldly similarity, from divine monarchy to human conformity. If the world is the contracting or unfolding of the absolute, then every part of the world is needed to complete the unfolding. Differences must flourish; each must be 'that which it is in the best way it can be',[15] valued not for its likeness to any another thing but as a unique and essential facet of the whole. For Nicholas, difference is non-competitive: it engenders not separation but mutuality. Each thing is what it is because of its relation to the whole: it is implicated in the whole. The theological principle of *perichoresis* or 'mutual interpenetration', originally a way of talking about the relations of the persons of the Holy Trinity, now describes all that exists: Nicholas draws close to what we would name an organic, holistic, ecological view of the world.

Just as Eckhart had understood that God cannot be simply transcendent, as if over against a bounded space that is 'ours', so Nicholas also sees that 'difference' cannot apply to God.[16] Neither, it follows, can 'sameness', because that is different from difference. Nicholas appeals to the Trinitarian nature of God as a beautiful model of 'otherness without otherness';[17] God who enfolds all things without otherness is 'the unity to which neither otherness nor plurality nor multiplicity is opposed'.[18]

We know only too well how easily such positive views of difference evaporate when things threaten to fall apart. Nicholas passed the test of his time. Already he had worked towards Catholic–Orthodox reunion, and in *On Learned Ignorance* he had applied the logic of his appreciation of difference to non-Christian faiths: 'the pagans themselves were worshipping God in God's unfoldings'.[19] He cited the temples of Peace, Eternity, Concord, and the Pantheon's altar 'dedicated to the Infinite Limit', recalling Paul's comments on the altar to the Unknown God in Athens (Acts 17.23). When, in 1453, Christian Constantinople fell to the Turks, rumours of bloody cruelties unleashed a wave of Islamophobia, compounding existing 'psychopathic forms of overexcited religiosity';[20] Pope Nicholas V called for a new crusade. Our Nicholas' response was a dream of peace: in *On the Peace of Faith* he imagines a great gathering, a feast, of men of different faiths. Catherine Keller notes:

> In context it is strange that the book never singles out its representatives of Islam as perpetrators. Rather, with tones of great respect, he includes a disproportionate number of Muslims in his imaginary – and in his time impossible – peace conference.[21]

As regards the use of affirmation and negation in theology, Nicholas faithfully follows Dionysius, whom he names the 'highest contemplator of the divine'.[22] All that exists is an 'unfolding' of the divine; all that is thought or said has some truth. Nothing is fully divine (the divine itself is no-thing); nothing thought or said is fully true. But like Eckhart before him, he searches out practical illustrations, everyday examples that will open up the apophatic wisdom beyond the theological academy. In the fateful year 1453 he fulfilled a promise to 'explain . . . the facility of mystical theology' to a monastic community, sending along with the text of *On the Vision of God* a painting, so that 'by means of a very simple and commonplace method I will attempt to lead you experientially into the most sacred darkness'.[23] We do not know exactly what the icon he sent looked like, but Nicholas describes it as an 'all-seeing face'. Hang it up, he tells the monks, and you will see that wherever you stand, the face seems to be looking at only you; and when you move, the eyes will seem to follow you. And if two of you move in different directions, it will seem to each of you that the eyes follow only you.

Nicholas' speculative venture in experimental theology yields a return that goes well beyond an understanding of perspective. That what we see depends on, and is relative to where we stand is already obvious from what he has established about unfolding and difference; now he draws the bolder conclusion that has been staring us in the face all this time.

First, and uncontroversially, we remember that God's gaze is creative, constitutive: 'I exist only insomuch as you are with me. And since your seeing is your being, therefore, because you regard me, I am, and if you remove your face from me, I will cease to be.'[24] The divine gaze is not only origin but also eschaton, not only creative but also restorative:

> Your seeing communicates your immortality and confers the imperishable glory of your heavenly and greatest kingdom. Moreover, it makes me partaker of that inheritance which is of the Son alone and renders me possessor of eternal happiness. Here is the source of all the delights that can be desired.[25]

Nicholas' apophatic strategy is to posit a picture on a wall and then direct our gaze away from it, away from what is represented, seen, conceived. Rather than to a subject seeing an object, Nicholas attends to the reality arising as relationship, in and through the mutual gaze. Here too there is a kind of interpenetration, a union of the non-different:

> What other, O Lord, is your seeing, when you look upon me with the eye of mercy, than your being seen by me? In seeing me you, who are the hidden God, give yourself to be seen by me. No one can see you except in the measure you grant to be seen. Nor is your being seen other than your seeing one who sees you.[26]

If, then, I only exist in the divine gaze, it follows that I cannot know who I am until I gaze upon God and meet divinity gazing at me. If I know nothing of God, I know nothing of myself or of the world that is given to me. Drawing Augustinian desire into Dionysian unknowing, Nicholas cries out:

> How will you give yourself to me if you do not at the same time give me heaven and earth and all that are in them? And, even more, how will you give me yourself if you do not also give me myself?

And when I rest thus in the silence of contemplation, you, Lord, answer me within my heart, saying: 'Be yours and I too will be yours.'[27]

The conclusion to this line of reasoning brings Nicholas once more within hailing-distance of many late twentieth-century theologies: the divinity I see is as shaped by my gaze as it in turn shapes me:

Whoever looks on you with a loving face will find only your face looking on oneself with love. And the more one strives to look on you with greater love, the more loving will one find your face. Whoever looks on you with anger will likewise find your face angry. Whoever looks on you with joy will also find your face joyous, just as is the face of the one who looks on you.[28]

No wonder, then, that this seeing and being seen is also a dark seeing, a clouded seeing. But before we enter the cloud with Nicholas, we need to make a small digression into the question of the divine name.

Nicholas recognizes, again following Dionysius, that God is both unnameable and known by a multitude of names. Kataphatically, 'since . . . God enfolds the whole of all things, it would be necessary either to assign every name to God or to call all things by God's name.' At the same time, the 'proper name' of God is the unsayable tetragrammaton revealed at the burning bush; it is 'no-name' and 'above all names'.[29] Nicholas, theologian, pastor and worshipper, continues to wrestle with Moses' question: if they ask me 'What is his name', what shall I say? 'Unity', or 'All in One', he suggests in *On Learned Ignorance*, or perhaps a Trinity of 'Unity, Itness and Sameness'.[30] Yet such names suggest too much, lean too far towards what 'is' at the expense of what is not, what might be, what is not yet: thus in 1460 he coins a new name, *Possest* – 'Can-Is'.

Nicholas' apophatic fuse was lit by a sudden divine vision on a ship. It seems that there was another such illumination later, perhaps in a nave. At Easter in 1464, the last year of his life, just after the vernal equinox, in who knows what pageantry of light, colour, perfume and song, we can surely assume that Bishop Nicholas celebrated a Eucharist of the Resurrection, and within a few days we know he laid hands to ordain his long-time secretary Peter of Erkelenz. Shortly thereafter a glorious final text emerged: the dialogue *On the Summit of Contemplation*. Peter opens proceedings in words that recall the beginning of *On the Hidden God*, quoted above: I can see, he says, that you are in deep meditation, and filled with joy, 'as if you had discovered some great thing'. Nicholas' reply cites St Paul, 'caught up to the third heaven' (2 Corinthians 12.2): this is not about understanding God, but being drawn deeper into the mystery. His eyes are opened afresh to the glory of God unfolding all around him, to wisdom 'shouting in the streets', and he has a new name for God: *Posse Ipsum*. *Posse* is the verb 'to be able': from its noun-form *potentia* we derive both 'potency' and 'potential'. After the liturgical proclamation and celebration of Christ's resurrection, the rebirth of life and joy after death and despair, the impossible made possible, Nicholas makes the short but significant journey from *Possest*, 'Can-Is', to 'Can Itself'. Overturning the weighty philosophical tradition that ever since Aristotle had subordinated 'potentiality' to 'actuality' and conceived of God as Supreme Being, Nicholas tenderly and joyously reconceives the omni-potence of God: no longer is it 'all power' to dominate and erase difference, but a fecund and inclusive 'all-possible': 'For all things are possible with God' (Mark 10.27).

Tangled up within the visual experiment of the 'all-seeing face' is a purely imaginative visual exercise. We follow Nicholas into the cloud of unknowing – or, as he also calls it, the cloud of impossibility – in a mood of worship and wonder:

> I thank you, my God, because you make clear to me that there is no other way of approaching you except that which to all humans, even to the most learned philosophers, seems wholly inaccessible and impossible. For you have shown me that you cannot be seen elsewhere than where impossibility confronts

and obstructs me. O Lord, you, who are the food of nature, have given me courage to do violence to myself, for impossibility coincides with necessity, and I have discovered that the place where you are found unveiled is girded about with the coincidence of contradictories.[31]

We find ourselves approaching Paradise – a walled garden within which the divine plays. The wall is the point, Nicholas says, where opposites coincide. Up to this point, finite and infinite, impossible and necessary, knowing and unknowing and all the rest of the dualistic-discriminative host are true antagonists. At the point of the wall they 'co-in-cide' – they *fall together, collapse in a heap.* (One wonders whether they in fact constitute the wall.) Not erased, not resolved, they are and are not, for 'in infinity contradiction is without contradiction because it is infinity'.[32] Somehow the wall must be breached, the door found and opened. The 'violence' required to effect the breach somehow implicates our very selves. Beyond, 'on the other side of the coincidence of contradictories', we meet the divine gaze in which our seeing is our being seen, our being seen is our being, and divine being seen is divine seeing.[33]

A different violence gathers as Nicholas makes his transit to glory. His struggles to reform the religious life of his diocese, and the ecclesial polity itself, are within a century to be swept up and away by a full-fledged Reformation and the Wars of Religion that come in its wake. Certainties compete and difference is to be erased. For several centuries, apophasis becomes an increasingly Nicodemite tradition. Was this what they tried to beat out of St John of the Cross? In schools of theology they ignored or tried to tame it: the negative way, a mostly harmless intellectual abstraction.

Nevertheless, for those with ears to hear, the possibility of the impossible continues to be proclaimed and celebrated every Christmas and Easter. The cloud of unknowing thickens into obscure but radiant flesh; divinity becomes human and humanity becomes divine; on a mountain-top Transfiguration *shows*, and on another mount a crossed tree bears the golden fruit of paradise; death gives birth. Nicholas, like Maximus before him, looks to a carpenter, an 'artisan', whom he tenderly calls 'good Jesus', 'my Jesus', in whom all contradictions find peace:

O Jesus, End of the universe, in whom every creature rests as in the ultimacy of perfection . . . you are the Tree of Life in the paradise of delights . . . Just as everyone is bound to you, O Jesus, by a human nature common to oneself and to you . . . everyone of happy spirit subsists in your Spirit, as the vivified in the vivifier. Every happy spirit sees the invisible God and is united in you, O Jesus, to the unapproachable and immortal God. And thus in you the finite is united to the infinite and to that which cannot be united, and the incomprehensible is seized by an eternal fruition, which is a most joyous and inexhaustible happiness. Have mercy, O Jesus, have mercy, and grant me to see you without veil, and my soul is saved![34]

Notes

1 The opening lines of Nicholas' *Dialogue on the Hidden God, in Nicholas of Cusa: Selected Spiritual Writings*, translated by H. L. Bond for the Classics of Western Spirituality series (New York: Paulist Press, 1997), p. 207.

2 Ibid., p. 207.

3 *On Learned Ignorance* I.5.14; Bond, p. 93.

4 Ibid. I.17.51; Bond, p. 110.

5 Ibid. I.19.55; Bond, p. 112.

6 Ibid. I.19.57; Bond, p. 113.

7 Ibid. I.26.87; Bond, p. 126.

8 Ibid. II.2.98 and II.4.112; Bond, pp. 131, 137.

9 Ibid. II.6.123; Bond, p. 142.

10 Ibid. II.11.161; Bond, p. 160. Nicholas expands further on the inadequacy of knowledge in *On Conjectures*, just a year or so later. It begins 'You have seen that the exactness of truth cannot be attained. The consequence is that every positive human assertion of the truth is a conjecture': *con-iecta*, 'thrown together', like a dart towards its target.

11 Ibid. III.181; Bond, p. 169.

12 Ibid. II.13.179; Bond, p. 168.

13 Ibid. III.12.258 and 262; Bond, pp. 203, 205.

14 Ibid. II.4.115 and II.5.117; Bond, pp. 139, 140.

15 Ibid. II.5.121; Bond, p. 142.

16 Ibid. II.1.91; Bond, p. 128.

17 *On the Vision of God* 17.75; Bond, p. 268.

18 *On Learned Ignorance* I.24.76; Bond, p. 121.

19 Ibid. I.25.83–4; Bond, pp. 124–5. Nicholas also notes with approval the pagan understanding that both masculinity and femininity must be enfolded within the divine character.

20 Erich Meuthen, *Nicholas of Cusa: A Sketch for a Biography*, translated by David Crowner and Gerald Christianson (Washington, DC: Catholic University of America Press, 2010), p. 16.

21 Catherine Keller, *Cloud of the Impossible: Negative Theology and Planetary Entanglement* (New York: Columbia University Press, 2015), p. 241.

22 *On Seeking God* III.46; Bond, p. 229.

23 *On the Vision of God* 1; Bond, p. 235.

24 Ibid. 4.10; Bond, p. 240.

25 Ibid. 4.12; Bond, pp. 240–1.

26 Ibid. 5.13; Bond, p. 241.

27 Ibid. 7.25; Bond, p. 247.

28 Ibid. 6.19; Bond, p. 243.

29 On *Learned Ignorance* I.24.75; Bond, p. 121.

30 Ibid. I.24.75 and I.9.25; Bond, pp. 121, 98.

31 *On the Vision of God* 9.37; Bond, pp. 251–2.

32 Ibid. 13.54; Bond, p. 259.

33 Ibid. 10.40; Bond, pp. 252–3.

34 Ibid. 21.91–4; Bond, pp. 276–8.

PART 4

Allies on the Journey

Carole Bury, 'Grace', charcoal.

Athens

Though we can from time to time trace the background influence of contemporary philosophies on biblical thought and language, there is only one place in the Bible where the wisdom of God is brought directly and explicitly into conversation with philosophers: Paul's missionary trip to Athens in Acts 17. We saw earlier that when a later Christian writer proclaimed gospel truth afresh in the philosophical language of his day, he chose to write under the name of Paul's Athenian convert, Dionysius the Areopagite. That Athens has become synonymous with secular wisdom and intellectual enquiry is largely the legacy of three men: Socrates, Plato and Aristotle. In the three centuries prior to the birth of Jesus of Nazareth their ideas had been carried by Hellenistic culture throughout the Mediterranean basin and through to the Indian subcontinent, leaving their mark on some of the later writings of the Jewish Scriptures and on the world of ideas in which Paul and many of his Gentile converts were formed.

Socrates, like Jesus, was a teacher in the oral tradition: he left no writings. We know about him from the records of his contemporaries. There is affectionate parody of him by the comic playwright Aristophanes, but for a detailed account of Socrates' ideas we rely almost entirely on the work of his pupil Plato. Socrates was by no means the first of the great Greek philosophers, but something quite distinctive happens as a result of his work: a change of direction in the history of philosophy that is often called 'the Socratic turn'. It seems that whereas (and of course this is a huge generalization) his predecessors were primarily interested in what we would call the natural sciences (that is, with investigating objective real-ity), Socrates began to ask systematic questions about how to live, whether and how we could know what is right or wrong – questions about ethics, politics, psychology and epistemology. The Socratic turn is towards a mirror, from a gaze bent on the world to a gaze directed towards our own minds and hearts.

Socrates' interest in distinguishing between second-hand opin-ions, the sort of thing people think they know because it is taken for granted in their home culture and because it suits them to believe it, and real knowledge, which is founded on evidence and can be backed up by reasoning, made him an irritant in Athens. Eventually he was accused of 'corrupting the minds of young people' and 'impiety', both of which amounted to the same thing: that he encouraged people to think for themselves, to doubt the received truth told by power-ful interests, to question the morality of state actions. According to Plato, the trouble began when an oracle described Socrates as 'the wisest man in Athens'. In Plato's account of his trial, Socrates gives a comic account of his perplexity at this, knowing how little wisdom he himself had; he embarks on a process of interviewing politicians, poets, playwrights and craftsmen, attempting to prove the oracle wrong by identifying someone wiser than himself. In each case he fails: those who think they are wise turn out only to trade on hand-me-down opinions or a sort of knack for their work. He concludes:

> The truth of the matter, gentlemen, is pretty certainly this: that real wisdom is the property of God, and this oracle is his way of telling us that human wisdom has little or no value. It seems to me that he is not referring literally to Socrates, but has merely taken my name as an example, as if he would say to us, 'The wisest of you men is he who has realized, like Socrates, that in respect of wisdom he is really worthless.'[1]

Thus Socrates establishes a paradoxical definition: to be wise is to know one's own ignorance.[2] Growth in wisdom is no longer sim-ply a matter of accruing 'facts'; an element of self-knowledge is required too, and this is acquired by stripping off all the opinions, prejudices and appearances in which we have wrapped ourselves, to see our own nakedness.

They found Socrates guilty, and he was executed.

Plato presents his work in dialogue form, not appearing as a character himself but putting the big ideas into Socrates' mouth. Increasingly, it seems that the views ascribed to Socrates are really Plato's, but it's hard to draw a precise line between them. Plato continues to hold up as a model the philosopher who searches for truth, for reality, and won't accept anything less. He had no difficulty in understanding how personally costly this commitment could be. In one of his mature works, *The Republic*, he sets out a programme for the establishment of a just society; it will be harmoniously ordered under the government of a ruling class of philosophers. (Plato is possibly the first exponent of the familiar idea that the only people who should be trusted with the power to govern are those who wouldn't want it.) These philosophers will rule justly because they are wise: they can see reality and they know goodness, and everything that flows from it.

Possibly the most famous passage in all Greek philosophy is the analogy Plato uses to explain how his philosophers will come to find truth: the Simile of the Cave. Imagine, he says, an underground path leading down into a natural cave. In the cave a whole society of people in chains are being brainwashed: the dim light of a fire is all they have, and they are chained up in such a way that they can't look at it directly. They are facing a wall, and all they can see are the shadows cast on the wall – silhouettes in the firelight of objects held up and manipulated by an unseen and unnamed elite. Without anything else to which to compare their experience, the prisoners understandably think that the cave is 'reality' and that the silhouettes are real objects.

Imagine further, Plato says, that somehow one prisoner becomes free of his chains. At first, when he turns around, the firelight will blind him. Finding it painful, he'll probably turn away from it and voluntarily stay with his fellows. But if he were made to take the path that leads upwards, the whole process would be repeated again as sunlight dawned at the end: he will again be blinded. Only very gradually will his eyes adjust. But what a scene can be imagined when at last he sees the world in all its glory and understands how false and fake was his earlier so-called 'knowledge'!

If such a man, once free, were to decide to go back into the cave and tell the truth to those who were still in chains, they would think him mad. His eyes would take a while to grow accustomed again to the dimness of the cave's light, and in that time the prisoners would see that he is a fool, because he would make all sorts of mistakes in identifying the things they count as real, and no doubt would stumble about in the dark and bump into them in the most irritating and foolish way. They would surely ignore him or try to silence him – or kill him.[3]

So when the great writers of the apophatic tradition talk of being stripped of what weighs us down, of leaving the world behind, of dazzling darkness and of the ascent into unknowing, they are not only making use of the images drawn from Exodus and the Song of Songs: all these themes are present in Plato's work.

All analogies have their limitations. One limitation of the Simile of the Cave is that it can make the journey towards knowledge seem rather like the journey envisaged by philosophers before the Socratic turn; as if it was simply objective scientific knowledge that was the goal. We need to look to other elements of Plato's work to round out our understanding. Plato's famous Theory of Forms expresses his conviction that there is a higher reality than our senses perceive, a reality available only to the mind. The broad distinction between 'the world of the senses' and the higher 'world of the mind' was simply part of the intellectual culture for most of the Christian centuries: it sits easily alongside the notion of an immaterial Creator of a material creation, and underlies a great deal of the writing of the apophatic tradition, such as the progression in negation through the final chapters of Dionysius' *Mystical Theology*.

Whereas science uses evidence and measurements derived from the senses to study the physical world, Plato's model of knowledge gives a higher value to mental faculties such as memory, reasoning and imagination. He suggests that our souls have seen non-material reality directly, before our birth, and that thereafter the process of education is really one of reminding people, helping them draw into consciousness the knowledge they carry within them.[4] Again, Plato's work is richly resonant to those who read it from the perspective of the apophatic tradition: the process of learning is a kind of stripping back. The proof that knowledge is innate within us is established by a slave-boy. Uneducated, he has not acquired all the usual layers of opinion and second-hand learning. It turns out, according to Plato, that true knowledge of reality comes hand in hand with knowledge of who we really are – that the 'beyondness of things' applies both to the perfect 'Forms' of all that is beautiful, true and good, and to ourselves.

Only a little less well known than the Simile of the Cave is a different analogy that immediately precedes it. Socrates has been trying to explain what the philosopher knows, what it is that makes him uniquely qualified to create a just and happy community. It is knowledge of Reality itself, called here the Form of the Good. He confesses that his ignorance means he cannot define it clearly, and offers a series of analogies instead – similes, stories, myths. In the Simile of the Divided Line he explains his view of the way we learn. There is the familiar distinction between opinion and knowledge: opinion is concerned with things we can learn through our senses, and therefore it is always at least second-hand, coming to the mind through unreliable organs such as eyes and ears, or very often third-hand or more, reported to us by someone who heard it from someone else who saw it and so on. Knowledge, on the other hand, is reliable because it is direct, unmediated: the mind perceives truth directly. But knowledge itself is subdivided into two categories. The details of Plato's text are very difficult to unpick here, but there seem to be two key points: the first is about the subject matter of the purest kind of knowledge, and the second is the way that knowing is achieved. Whereas you can get to the lower kind of knowledge by a process of abstraction (starting from sense perception and stripping away all that is unreliable or variable, working towards a reasoned conclusion), the higher kind of knowledge is able to uncover 'first principles', the underlying patterns and structures of reality. And how that true knowing is achieved is suggested in the name Plato gives to it: *dialectic*. The 'power of dialectic', he insists, is what unlocks the 'ascent' to the 'first principle of everything'.[5]

Like the Cave, the Simile of the Divided Line makes the ascent to knowledge a key theme, and its concomitant process of learning to distrust or lay aside what we once thought to be true. But the Line's stress on dialectic is distinctive and worth dwelling on. Dialectic is a fundamentally conversational process: it might be a conversation one has entirely within oneself, though it belongs most naturally in a community because it is a process of revolving and analysing ideas ('If we say x, then y logically follows; and if y, then z . . .'), discarding some, refining others. It's the process of doubting and discussing, of subjecting absolutely everything to critical examination, that Plato marks out as the only thing that can lead us to Reality itself, the source of all life and goodness and beauty.

If you take Plato at his word and subject his analogies to critical discussion, one of the biggest issues to emerge concerns the relationship between the ascending progression, through learning and unlearning, to knowledge, and the goal of the ascent, the source of all, which he calls the Form of the Good. Put simply, sometimes it seems that the ascent gets you to the Form of the Good, but at other times it seems that the highest place it can get you to is still not the Form of the Good itself, which remains 'beyond'. Like a ship's pilot who can see the stars and navigate by their light, but not touch them, perhaps the philosopher in the end has arrived in the place where the source of all might be most closely encountered, but not comprehended. Plato's use of the analogy with the sun means that there is no darkness at the top of his ascent, though he has noted how blindingly dazzling light can be until we are accustomed to it. Nevertheless, there does seem to be a resonance with Moses standing in the cloud at the top of Sinai: God, the Good, reality, the source of all, is both present and ungraspable.

The dominant theme of Plato's argument is that the true philosopher will know the Good itself. Similarly, Moses does encounter God and the holy name is disclosed: 'I AM'. This led to an equally dominant emphasis in Christian tradition that later thinkers call 'ontotheology': God is identified with pure being, not 'a being' but Being itself.

Yet undeniably present in Plato, albeit as a minor theme, is an idea that gets close to a philosophical version of nuclear fission. Likening the Form of the Good to the sun, which is both visible itself but also the source of the life of all visible things, and therefore far beyond them, he says that 'the good is not being, but beyond and superior to being in dignity and power.'[6] The sheer beyondness of the source takes precedence even over its beingness: the source of all is 'beyond being'. The implications of this are worked out by Plato's later successors, most notably the third-century Plotinus, and reverberated in the development of Christian apophatic spirituality. For the name disclosed to Moses on Sinai is also no-name. Does it reserve 'being' to itself, or set itself above 'being'?

Gregory of Nyssa might in theory have arrived at his insights about the complete beyondness of God, and the infinite progression in spiritual fulfilment, simply by contemplating his Bible and his experience of Christian living; so too the author of the Dionysian corpus, who begins *The Mystical Theology* with a prayer to the Trinity 'higher than any being, any divinity, any goodness'. In fact these thinkers are undeniably shaped by the Greek intellectual culture of their day; this is part of what it means for God's truth always to be incarnated, located within a particular person and his/her perspective. With Athens as an ally, these Christian thinkers were confident in developing a theology that understands even our notions of divinity, being and goodness as *notions*, falling short of holy reality. Their exploration of the possibility of a faith free even of 'ontotheology' is one of the most exciting elements of our inherited faith being taken up in contemporary theology and spirituality, as we seek in a postmodern context to speak of God 'as he is'.

The vast influence that Aristotle – the third of the Athenian greats – has had on the development of Western Christian theology is mainly in areas other than the apophatic. We need to pause only briefly, therefore, to note his discussion of the nature of God and of the best life for humanity. One of the most attractive things about Aristotle's philosophy is his deep understanding of the social nature of humanity, leading to an appreciation of individual friendships and of the importance of citizenship. He endeavours to hold together both the Greek insights about intellectual and spiritual ascent to the 'beyond', and a much more positive assessment of our common life than we might read off Plato's description of life in the cave. Discussing the nature of the cause of all things, Aristotle, in Book 12 of his *Metaphysics*, echoes the consensus that our first job if we are to think seriously about God is to strip away all the unsuitable ideas that are part of popular religion. Then he goes on to consider what can be said about the divine mind; he struggles to articulate a kind of perfect consciousness that is beyond all that we normally associate with thinking and not-thinking. When he turns to consider the best kind of human life, without disregarding all that is good in the practical and material realm, he becomes almost wistful:

> Any man who lives [a life of perfect happiness] will do so not as a human being but in virtue of something divine within him ... we ought, so far as in us lies, to put on immortality, and do all that we can to live in conformity with the highest that is in us ... Indeed it would seem that this is the true self of the individual ...[7]

The means whereby we 'put on immortality' is to share, in so far as we are able, in the perfect consciousness of the divine mind. Aristotle, following tradition, calls this *theoria*, 'contemplation'. It is the Greek word that many of the Christian spiritual writers later used for the highest form of prayer, 'pure prayer' – prayer that is not filled with words or with thinking about this or that, or even with trying not to think, but with a simple receptive awareness, waiting for the touch of the beloved.

All of this – the ascent, the progress in knowledge towards a dazzling light, the setting aside of hearsay in the search for direct encounter with a reality that is utterly beyond, even beyond being itself, the belief that in contemplating as God contemplates we find our own truest selves – all of this is the backdrop to St Paul's encounter with the philosophical and spiritual enquirers of Athens, who asked him to explain his teachings:

> So Paul, standing in the midst of the Areopagus, said: 'Men of Athens, I perceive that in every way you are very religious. For as I passed along and observed the objects of your worship, I found also an altar with this inscription, 'To an unknown god.' (Acts 17.22–23)

Paul goes on to identify the Athenians' unknown god as the God who is the source of all, beyond all and utterly close to all. He quotes their own literature to secure this identification (17.28). And on this basis, we are told, some Athenians 'joined him and believed', including 'Dionysius the Areopagite and a woman named Damaris and others' (17.34). We might possibly think that Paul is simply filling the Athenians in on something they had not known: 'You worship a God who you do not know, and I can tell you who he is . . .' But perhaps that's not what he meant. Perhaps the point is that Athens, like Jerusalem, knows that there is a God beyond all knowing; that Jesus and his message of the kingdom is the best and clearest signpost we will ever have, pointing to the Father who:

> made the world and everything in it, being Lord of heaven and earth . . . And he made from one man every nation of mankind to live on all the face of the earth . . . that they should seek God, in the hope that they might feel their way towards him and find him. (Acts 17.24–27)

Notes

1 Plato, 'The Apology of Socrates', in *The Last Days of Socrates*, translated by H. Tredennick (London: Penguin, 1959), p. 52.

2 This 'Socratic ignorance' was later utilized by Nicholas of Cusa in support of his argument that not only God but all created things flowing from him are ultimately unknowable – *On Learned Ignorance* I.1.4, in *Nicholas of Cusa: Selected Spiritual Writings*, translated by H. L. Bond for the Classics of Western Spirituality series (New York: Paulist Press, 1997), p. 88.

3 The Simile of the Cave is in Book 7 of Plato's *Republic*, sections 514–7; and pp. 316–20 of Tredennick's translation for Penguin Classics.

4 The famous demonstration that knowledge is remembered is in Plato's *Meno*; his theory about pre-incarnate knowledge is set out in mythical form in the last book of *The Republic*.

5 The Simile of the Divided Line is at the end of Book 6 of Plato's *Republic*, sections 509d–511e; and pp. 310–16 of Tredennick's translation for Penguin Classics.

6 The Republic, 509b – my translation.

7 Aristotle, *The Nicomachean Ethics* 1177b–1178a; cited in J. A. K. Thomson's translation for Penguin Classics (London, 2004, revised edition), p. 272.

Keats' Negative Capability

Over Christmas of the year 1817, the 22-year-old poet John Keats wrote a newsy letter to his younger brothers George and Tom. He talked of dramatic performances and art exhibitions, of company pleasant and tedious, of walks and plans – the sort of daily trivia we nowadays share on social media. Towards the end of the letter he reflects on a conversation during a walk with a friend:

> at once it struck me, what quality went to form a Man of Achievement especially in Literature & which Shakespeare possessed so enormously – I mean *Negative Capability*, that is when a man is capable of being in uncertainties, Mysteries, doubts, without any irritable reaching after fact & reason – Coleridge, for example, would let go by a fine isolated verisimilitude caught from the Penetralium of mystery, from being incapable of remaining content with half knowledge. This pursued through Volumes would perhaps take us no further than this, that with a great poet the sense of Beauty overcomes every other consideration, or rather obliterates all consideration.[1]

Although to our knowledge he never used the phrase itself again, 'negative capability' has become widely celebrated. It seems to capture something essential not just to Keats' own poetic vocation but to creative thinking, artistic process and human development in wisdom. Keats' insight has been identified with highly complex aesthetic philosophy on the one hand, and reduced to cliché on the other: 'Live the questions'. Many have also noted how close Keats is here to the apophatic tradition, including among recent writers Catherine Keller, Maggie Ross and Richard Kearney, for example:

There is but a thin line . . . separating Keats' formula of literary agnosticism from the analogous moves of apophatic mysticism in theology or the methodic suspension of accredited certainties in philosophy. And perhaps a certain poetics of negative capability is at the heart of all religious and philosophical exposures to 'the strange'? For it is surely such exposure which prompts us to begin all over again, to surrender inherited sureties and turn towards the Other – in wonder and bewilderment, in fear and trembling, in fascination and awe.[2]

Kearney and others suggest that Keats identifies an attitude, a way of being in the world, that makes both his own poetry and – if he is right – creative thought in general natural allies of apophatic spirituality. We'll explore three characteristics of this attitude.

First, the poet is another one who notices burning bushes by the way and strips off all protecting layers in order to approach them.

Just as 'negative theology' is not *simply* negative – not about smashing all words and images of God and leaving the pieces lying around, but about feeding on the words and images, then clearing them away, and then going beyond both the images and the clearing away – so in the same way Keats' 'negative capability' is not *simply* negative. Keats isn't talking about a lazy or sleepy passivity, lolling around in 'uncertainties, Mysteries, doubts', with the sort of voluptuous languor of a 'dull brain' suggested in his 'Ode to a Nightingale'. The passivity he has in mind takes courage: it is an open receptivity, a willingness to bear the direct impressions of reality without protecting ourselves by interposing layers of interpretative thought. In an earlier letter to Benjamin Bailey he had mused:

I have never yet been able to perceive how any thing can be known for truth by consequitive reasoning . . . sure this cannot be exactly the case with . . . the philosophic Mind – such an one I consider your's and therefore it is necessary to your eternal Happiness that you not only drink this old Wine of Heaven which I shall call the redigestion of our most ethereal Musings on Earth; but also increase in knowledge and know all things.[3]

Keats' 'philosophic Mind' must know all things: negative capability is about a spacious mind, not an empty one. The contrast is not so much between 'uncertainty' and 'fact and reason' but between the two attitudes of mind, 'capability' and 'irritable reaching'. His biographer Stephen Coote has traced some of the tributary streams of thought that meet in negative capability: they include critical theory, artistic performance (Keats admired the 'gusto' of actors who could convey a character with intense immediacy) and science – Keats had been training to be an apothecary:

> the choice of the word 'negative' almost certainly derives from Keats' chemistry lectures, where negativity implied not a rejection, a minus or an absence, but rather a sympathetic receptive intensity. Just as, for Bailey, Keats had compared the actions of great minds to catalysts, so, for his brothers, he could imply that the 'negative capability' of the true poet was like an electrical negative: passive but, in its receptive power, quite the equal of the positive current.[4]

If Coote is right, then the mind of one who is 'negatively capable' is like an exposed wire or open terminal. A more traditional image of receptivity might have been the wax in which a seal can be impressed – but that image is also static, lacking the energy, the electricity of Keats' chosen image. In another celebrated phrase, Keats wrote that 'axioms in philosophy are not axioms until they are proved upon our pulses.'[5] This 'proving' of axioms is reminiscent of Plato's 'dialectic', suggesting both the immediacy of personal experience and also a form of cognition that is not 'consequitive' but pulsing, with a rhythm of expansion and contraction. We are not very far from the apophatic rhythm of knowing-and-unknowing.

Second, Keats' artist has an 'anagogic' function. Art aspires to present the intense heart of experience. If we can bear – if we are 'capable' of receiving – the weight of vivid particulars without imposing our own intellectual programme on them, the mind may be initiated into 'Mystery'. Just before the remark about negative capability, Keats reports his reaction to a painting, Benjamin West's *Death on a Pale Horse*: 'There is nothing to be intense upon; no women one feels mad to kiss; no face swelling into reality . . .'[6] Rather than exhibiting the coolness of the stereotypical detached contemplative, for Keats the artist should feed upon sensual detail, just as the author(s) of the Song of Songs had. And just as in the Song, this is not the end of the matter: through such 'verisimilitude' the artist 'catches' something from 'the Penetralium of Mystery' – something that opens the mind to beauty, the presence of the beloved.

Keats offers his own version of the mind's ascent in a famous simile, taken from the same letter as the philosophical 'pulse':

> I compare human life to a large Mansion of Many Apartments, two of which I can only describe, the doors of the rest being as yet shut upon me – The first we step into we call the infant or thoughtless Chamber, in which we remain as long as we do not think . . . but are at length imperceptibly impelled by the awakening of the thinking principle – within us – we no sooner get into the second Chamber, which I shall call the Chamber of Maiden-Thought, than we become intoxicated with the light and the atmosphere, we see nothing but pleasant wonders, and think of delaying there ever in delight: However among the effects this breathing is father of is that tremendous one of sharpening one's vision into the heart and nature of Man – of convincing one's nerves that the World is full of Misery and Heartbreak, Pain, Sickness and oppression – whereby this Chamber of Maiden Thought becomes gradually darken'd and at the same time on all sides of it many doors are set open – but all dark – all leading to dark passages – We see not the ballance of good and evil. We are in a Mist.[7]

Like John of the Cross and Maximus the Confessor before him, Keats does not need to give a formal role in our ascent to an intellectual discipline of casting off beliefs: he understands that experienced suffering tends to do this quite naturally for sensitive minds. Living for so long the appalling half-life of sickrooms in which first his mother and then his brother Tom died of consumption, and under a repressive regime of violent reaction in England to the intellectual freedoms of the Enlightenment and the social and political experiments following the French Revolution, Keats knew nothing so clearly as that all 'received wisdom', all grand theory and presumed certainty, was a trap for coward minds. He wrote to Benjamin Bailey, 'You know my ideas about Religion – I do not think myself more in the right than other people and that nothing in this world is proveable',[8] and in similar vein to his brother George and his wife Georgiana, in the poignant letter in which he tells them of their brother Tom's last moments, assuring them of his 'scarce doubt' of some form of immortality:

> The more we know the more inadequacy we discover in the world to satisfy us . . . I have made up my Mind never to take anything for granted – but even to examine the truth of the commonest proverbs.[9]

The intoxicating light and the terrifying dark passages of the Chamber of Maiden Thought together create a swirling and disorientating mist in which vision is tentative at best. Although he claims only to be able to describe the first two chambers of this Mansion, Keats dared to offer a tender prophecy for his sick friend Reynolds: 'Your third Chamber of Life shall be a lucky and a gentle one – stored with the wine of love – and the Bread of Friendship.'[10] The eucharistic imagery is unmistakable.

Third, negative capability demands that in order to be fully alive to reality, the mind must free itself as much as possible from attachment to a fixed 'self'. Keats recognizes that fixed opinions express, shape and fortify our identities, and that opinion and identity are stripped off together. Bad art, like bad politics, seeks to dominate and impose – he refers to the 'wordsworthian or egotistical sublime' in a letter to Richard Woodhouse that contains his clearest explanation of the 'poetical Character':

> it is not itself – it has no self – it is everything and nothing – It has no character . . . A Poet is the most unpoetical of any thing in existence; because he has no Identity – he is continually in for – and filling some other Body.[11]

In contrast to the fixed and imposed identity shored up by views and certainties, Keats in another letter to George and Georgiana sets out an account of the world as a 'Vale of Soul-Making', in which a true identity emerges gradually, hard-won by struggle, responsive and 'formed by circumstances'. He offers this account as 'a grander system of salvation than the chrystain religion', though not very far removed from the approach of many theologians, and reminiscent of Eckhart's 'Godhead beyond God'.[12]

Ultimately, negative capability for Keats is not simply a theory about poetic creativity: it is about how we develop 'the philosophic Mind' in its truest and most literal sense, a mind that 'loves wisdom'. It is a theory for all of us as potential 'Men [and women] of Achievement', about how we can cast off false, damaged and damaging identities along with the supposed knowledge that undergirds them, and grow into an authentic self that sees reality as it is, and the Reality beyond it. The affinity between Keats' work and the apophatic tradition – within and beyond the Christian writers – is noted by Iain McGilchrist in his extraordinary account of our divided brain and its implications for human flourishing.[13]

McGilchrist's painstaking and complex analysis, based on experimental research, shows that the two hemispheres of our brain, broadly speaking, interact differently with the world of experience. The left hemisphere imposes order by naming, distinguishing, analysing, manipulating and generally by fitting sense-data into theories. It is this hemisphere that clarifies, seeks certainty and in Keats' words is 'intoxicated with the light'. The right hemisphere is more holistic, intuitive; McGilchrist describes it as 'apparently passive', open 'to whatever is', without a desire to control it.

As regards experience, the left hemisphere 're-presents' experience to us, sorted and categorized to suit our (its?) own purposes, with a neat interpretative overlay, like the impression we get of Othello in Shakespeare's first scene. It tells us that we know. It builds the theoretical frameworks that we need to use for everyday functioning, but they are always simplifications and therefore to a greater or lesser extent falsifications. In McGilchrist's words, such interpretative overlays 'veil' reality.[14]

The right hemisphere, on the other hand, is simply present to experience, like the way we encounter Othello for ourselves in the second scene of the play, our attention caught by the vitality of the man and his integrity of word and action. Though the right hemisphere has no 'design' on reality, it is not exactly neutral with regard to it: it has 'a relationship of concern or care . . . with whatever happens to be' – in other words, there is a sort of personal commitment that goes hand in hand with 'being content with a degree of *not*-knowing':[15]

> This nugatory or apophatic mode of creation of whatever-it-is is reflected in our experience that what we *know* about things as they truly are, starting with Being itself, is apophatic in nature: we can *know* only what they are *not*. Its particular significance is that it describes the path taken to truth by the right hemisphere, which sees things whole, and if asked to describe them has to remain 'silent'.[16]

McGilchrist explicitly describes his model of the mind's working in apophatic terms, using language of veiling, stripping, sculpting and chiselling. The two modes of experience are in a way just that: parallel or alternative processes. But he has no doubt that the right hemisphere, the one with 'negative capability', must retain a degree of primacy over the other. His verdict is that:

> Ultimately we need to unite the ways of seeing that are yielded by both hemispheres. Above all the attention of the left hemisphere needs to be reintegrated with that of the right hemisphere if it is not to prove damaging.[17]

McGilchrist, like Keats and Kearney, is talking about our experience of 'reality' in general rather than specifically of 'God', of course; we cannot simply claim that they are talking about the same thing as the Christian apophatic tradition. But in their recognition that our sanity, our identity and our capacity to find meaning and delight in

life depend on our being 'capable of being in uncertainties', they are
powerful allies.

Through the last two years before his death at the age of just 25,
Keats struggled to compose an epic poem that would depict personal, cultural and spiritual growth, his vision of the 'Vale of Soul-
Making', through a treatment of the displacement and replacement
of gods. Building imaginatively on Greek myth, Keats told of the
defeat of Saturn's Titans and their replacement by Zeus' Olympians.
The poem exists in two incomplete versions, both exploring the
development of negative capability through awareness of suffering;
the apophatic themes of ascent, veiling and stripping off, uncertainty and change are more fully developed in the later draft.

Keats' first version of the poem, published as *Hyperion: A
Fragment*, 'begins', as Coote says, 'in silence and ends with a scream'.[18]
It was begun in September 1818, while nursing Tom through his
last illness, and given up the following spring. The fallen Titans'
pain and confusion are tenderly and vividly expressed; these gods
are not simply symbols of the political and cultural forces whose
downfall Keats would heartily have celebrated, but have also pre-
sided over beauty, stability and order – Saturn sees his authority
as benign, peaceful and issuing from a 'heart of love' (*Hyperion*, ll.
108–112). True to his own principles, Keats catches from the sen-
sory details of his own experience an insight into 'Mystery': we can
imagine what Keats the physician saw before him as he described a
God whose awareness of his own doom 'made his hands to struggle
in the air, His Druid locks to shake and ooze with sweat, His eyes to
fever out, his voice to cease' (ll. 136–8). The burning core of this version, though, is the fall of the old sun-god Hyperion and the rise of
his successor, Apollo. Hyperion is glorious but he sees through his
own eyes only and cannot bend to change. Apollo, who will bring
poetry, music and art with him to solar status, gains through his
capacity for sympathetic sorrow a 'knowledge enormous' (l. 113,
recalling the Philosophic mind, above, which 'knows all things').
He becomes a God, in Keats' extraordinary depiction, not by gentle

transfiguration but painfully, by something like a death to his former self.

By summer 1819, Keats was working on a second version of the poem, again never completed: this time an additional dimension was added, a narrator who ascends to a vision of these events. Where the earlier draft appeared to give a straightforward description of events, the later version makes explicit the subjective and uncertain perspective of the poet-narrator, with all its frailties. This time the poem's title is *The Fall of Hyperion: A Dream,* and its opening lines surrender to later readers the task of judging its truth or falsity. As he wrestles to distinguish 'dreaming' from poetry, false enchantment from true 'imagination' (ll. 1–11), a struggle in which the poet's own life is at stake (ll. 107ff.), Keats holds fast to an insight shared with Gregory, Eckhart, John and Nicholas – that the yardstick of truth is measured in sympathetic love and a capacity to heal:

> . . . sure not all
> Those melodies sung into the world's ear
> Are useless: sure a poet is a sage,
> A humanist, physician to all men.[19]

In the earlier version, the Titan Oceanus is given the words that express Keats' evolutionary hope, that it is 'Nature's law' (II.181) and 'naked truth' (II.203) that in time all powers are unfixed and fall:

> So on our heels a fresh perfection treads,
> A power more strong in beauty, born of us
> And fated to excel us, as we pass
> In glory that old Darkness.[20]

Now with dramatic irony the deposed Saturn calls for his successors to suffer the same fate: 'Throw down those imps' (I.431). The poet has believed before that however painful the process, the dethronement of old certainties is an upwards step towards the Third Chamber of Life; but this too is interpretation, and therefore vulnerable.

Keats was shortly to face his own death, in fevered pain and disappointment, his earlier hope in some form of immortality seeming to slip away. He was, at least in part, wrong. The earlier version of his poem ends with lines describing the ascent to divinity of his own patron Apollo:

> Soon wild commotions shook him, and made flush
> All the immortal fairness of his limbs –
> Most like the struggle at the gate of death;
> Or liker still to one who should take leave
> Of pale immortal death, and with a pang
> As hot as death's is chill, with fierce convulse
> Die into life . . .[21]

The young poet too, devoted visionary of truth and beauty, eaten up from within by tuberculosis, far from home and loves, pale and convulsed, died into life.

Notes

1 Robert Gittings, *Letters of John Keats* (Oxford: Oxford University Press, 1970), p. 43.

2 Richard Kearney, *Anatheism: Returning to God After God* (New York: Columbia University Press, 2010), p. 11; see also Catherine Keller, *Cloud of the Impossible: Negative Theology and Planetary Entanglement* (New York: Columbia University Press, 2015), p. 5; Maggie Ross, *Silence: A User's Guide* (London: Darton, Longman & Todd, 2014), p. 29.

3 Letter to Benjamin Bailey, 22 November 1817, Gittings, pp. 37–8.

4 Stephen Coote, *John Keats: A Life* (London: Hodder & Stoughton, 1995), p. 116.

5 Letter to J. H. Reynolds, 3 May 1818, Gittings, p. 93.

6 Gittings, p. 42.

7 Gittings, p. 95.

8 13 March 1818, Gittings, pp. 72–3.

9 At the turn of the year 1818/9, Gittings, p. 187.

10 Gittings, p. 96.

11 27 October 1818, Gittings, p. 157.

12 April 1819, Gittings, pp. 249–51.

13 Iain McGilchrist, *The Master and his Emissary: The Divided Brain and the Making of the Western World* (New Haven, CT: Yale University Press, 2009).

14 Ibid., p. 173.

15 Ibid., p. 175; emphasis original.

16 Ibid., p. 197; emphasis original.

17 Ibid., p. 174.
18 Coote, p. 200.
19 *The Fall of Hyperion: A Dream*, ll. 187–90.
20 *Hyperion: A Fragment* II.212–16.
21 Ibid. III.124–30.

Narnia

At Evensong on 8 June 1941, in Oxford's University Church, a layman with no formal theological training preached what has been described as 'one of the most important sermons of the twentieth century'. That layman was C. S. Lewis; his sermon, titled 'The Weight of Glory', was published in 1942 and is still in print over 75 years later.[1]

Lewis began his sermon by reflecting on the nature of desire. Rather than warning against the intoxications of earthly desires and exhorting his audience to seek the 'narrow way' of spiritual discipline leading to heavenly glory, Lewis encouraged them to be bolder in their desires:

> Our Lord finds our desires, not too strong, but too weak. We are half-hearted creatures, fooling about with drink and sex and ambition when infinite joy is offered us, like an ignorant child who wants to go on making mud pies in a slum because he cannot imagine what is meant by the offer of a holiday at the sea. We are far too easily pleased.

In Christian infancy, Lewis argued, it may seem that we are asked to give up certain pleasures because they appear as rivals to our desire for God. We may even be afraid to desire God, suspicious 'lest it should be a mercenary desire'. But as we grow we find that our capacity for desire grows, and with it our confidence in desiring. The sweetness of created things becomes somehow transparent as we realize that our deepest longing is not for them but for something beyond, glimpsed through them.

Lewis reflected on what happens when we attempt to speak of the heart's deepest longing:

In speaking of this desire for our own far-off country, which we find in ourselves even now, I feel a certain shyness. I am almost committing an indecency. I am trying to rip open the inconsolable secret in each one of you – the secret which hurts so much . . . which pierces with such sweetness that when, in very intimate conversation, the mention of it becomes imminent, we grow awkward and affect to laugh at ourselves; the secret we cannot hide and cannot tell, though we desire to do both. We cannot tell it because it is a desire for something that has never actually appeared in our experience. We cannot hide it because our experience is constantly suggesting it, and we betray ourselves like lovers at the mention of a name.

Lewis neither claimed to be a mystic nor offered an explicitly apophatic understanding of the life of faith. His first university appointment, however, was as a tutor in philosophy, and from 1925 until his death in 1963 he taught English Literature, specializing in the medieval and Renaissance periods. He knew his Plato and Keats; he knew the work of Dionysius and *The Cloud of Unknowing* and was expert in the culture within which Marguerite Porete, Meister Eckhart and Nicholas of Cusa wrote.[2] He read with great appreciation the American monk Thomas Merton, one of the twentieth century's most significant explorers and teachers of the apophatic tradition.[3]

At the time he preached 'The Weight of Glory', the germ of an idea about a book for children was already in Lewis' mind; but the Narnia Chronicles did not come to fruition for some years afterwards: starting with *The Lion, the Witch and the Wardrobe*, the seven books were written in the years 1948–54.

Peter, Susan, Edmund and Lucy Pevensey discover a country that is in some ways 'far off', so far that it is normally inaccessible. There, through adventure and essentially through their encounters with the lion Aslan, 'the King of the wood and the son of the great Emperor-beyond-the-Sea', they learn the truth about themselves and become kings and queens. Thereafter Narnia is for ever their

'own far-off country'. At the same time it is very close by – an intimately 'private and secret country'[4] that can be entered through a
wardrobe door, a picture on a wall in an ordinary room or just by
sitting in a railway carriage.

While it would be silly and misleading to call the Chronicles of
Narnia 'apophatic texts' (just about as misleading as describing
Aslan as a 'talking lion'), in them Lewis weaves a glorious extended
imaginative parable whose fabric includes familiar apophatic
themes. Throughout the Chronicles he fleshes out the analysis
in 'The Weight of Glory' of longing, transposing into children's
fiction the insights of St John of the Cross and others. In Alister
McGrath's summary: 'Desire can become a semiotic barrier to the
discovery of God, if we try to follow it, assuming it is the true
object of longing, when it is merely a sign of a more distant goal.'[5]
Events in Narnia show how our desires, if we fix them on something less than that 'more distant goal', can grow into monstrous
idols, distorting us into lesser versions of ourselves, eventually
subsuming us under the idol's nature. Thus Edmund's fancy for
Turkish Delight, when fed by the White Witch, leaves him 'snap-
pish . . . flushed and strange'. His will is suborned: Turkish Delight
is no longer one of many treats to be enjoyed but the only thing.
Dominated by this longing he 'was already more than half on the
side of the Witch'; a boy with a capacity for spitefulness becomes
a heedless traitor.[6] Later, Prince Rilian's longing to avenge his
mother drives him into the snares of the Serpent-Witch; Eustace's
self-centred desire for superiority turns him into a dragon; Lucy
is almost defeated by a longing to be 'beautiful beyond the lot of
mortals'.[7]

Once Edmund has encountered Aslan, fought and broken the
witch's wand and 'become his real old self again', we see what true,
honest desire is like. Upon the children's enthronement at Cair
Paravel 'there was a great feast . . . and revelry and dancing, and gold
flashed and wine flowed'; whether or not there was Turkish Delight
on the tables we are not told, though it would be hard to imagine a really good feast without it. It doesn't matter enough now to
need mention. What earlier on appeared to be rival desires – either
Turkish Delight or fidelity – are now reconciled; within the rule
of Aslan all other good things are restored to us. (Even confused

and mistaken desires are purified and fulfilled: Emeth the young Calormene finds his longing for the 'true' god Tash fulfilled when he meets Aslan.[8]) By the time 'the White Stag who would give you wishes if you caught him' appears in Narnia, Edmund has thoroughly learned his lesson – that 'to go from all to the all you must deny yourself of all in all'. Despite the stirring foreboding in their hearts, the Pevensies set aside the wonders of Narnia to follow this rare and elusive symbol of beauty beyond all that they already possess, as Edmund declares: 'I have such desire to find the signification of this thing that I would not by my good will turn back for the richest jewel in all Narnia and all the islands.'[9]

Although the unblushingly erotic imagery of desire in the Song of Songs would not fit into the Narnia Chronicles, there are delicate hints in Prince Caspian's urgent desire to kiss – and later marry – Ramandu's daughter, at whose first appearance 'they thought they had never before known what beauty meant'.[10] Rowan Williams notes the 'strong endearments', containing 'something very like an erotic charge', with which Aslan speaks to those who encounter him: they are 'sweetheart', 'Dear Heart', 'Dearest'; and also 'the strong kisses of a king, and . . . wild kisses of a lion' exchanged by Caspian and Aslan.[11]

The end of all our longing is not merely to encounter God but to be united with him. Eckhart and St John of the Cross both acknowledge that a basic kind of union is essential to life itself; Lewis captures this basic union in Aslan's revivifying the White Queen's statues – giants, fauns, lions and all kinds come back to glowing vibrant life as the lion breathes on them. Like Gregory of Nyssa and the author of *The Cloud of Unknowing*, he presents a more significant union as loss of the 'small self' through active participation: when Aslan tells Lucy that she must play her part in the defeat of Narnia's enemies:

> Lucy buried her head in his mane to hide from his face. But there must have been magic in his mane. She could feel lion-strength going into her. Quite suddenly she sat up. 'I'm sorry, Aslan,' she said, 'I'm ready now.'
> 'Now you are a lioness,' said Aslan. 'And now all Narnia will be renewed.'[12]

In 'The Weight of Glory' Lewis had already identified the paradox of holy longing: that the more it is satisfied the more it grows.
When Lucy notices that Aslan has 'got bigger', he responds: 'Every
year you grow, you will find me bigger.'[13] The scale of the distance
or difference between the child and the lion will never be dimin-
ished. This is the truth of Moses encountering only the 'back parts'
of God (Exodus 33.23) and of Gregory of Nyssa's *epektasis*; it is the
apophatic insistence on the infinite beyondness of God. Even in
union, God cannot be fully known. The call of the mouse at the
end of it all is to 'come further up and further in' to a land that is
more and more real, and Mr Tumnus confirms the holy truth: 'The
further up and the further in you go, the bigger everything gets. The
inside is larger than the outside.'[14]

Aslan is both known in encounter and essentially unknowable and
unpredictable: hence the repeated admonitions that he is neither
'tame' nor 'safe'. Kallistos Ware calls him 'a profoundly apophatic
lion', and points to this exchange:

> 'I think you've seen Aslan,' said Edmund . . .
> 'But who is Aslan?' [asked Eustace] 'Do you know him?'
> 'Well – he knows me,' said Edmund.[15]

In one episode Lewis combines echoes of God's declaration 'I am
who I am' at the burning bush and Elijah's mountain-top encounter with 'the still small voice'. The boy Shasta has been 'stalked' by a
terrifying 'Thing' and at last summons the courage to speak:

> 'Who *are* you?' asked Shasta?
> 'Myself,' said the voice, very deep and low so that the earth shook
> again. 'Myself', loud and clear and gay: and then the third time
> 'Myself', whispered so softly you could hardly hear it . . .[16]

Throughout the Narnia Chronicles, 'Aslan' is used as if it were the
lion's name, but it too is not quite a name: Lewis simply took the
Turkish word for 'lion'.

Allegiance to Aslan throws a great deal else into doubt. The children are presented with puzzles, with clues whose significance is unclear, with contradictory stories, with dreams and nightmares that threaten to become horribly real, and realities that threaten to dissolve into dream. Assumptions are challenged and subverted. When Lucy first encounters Mr Tumnus it is the human girl and not the Narnian faun that is an almost impossible creature: on his bookshelf is the splendidly titled *Is Man a Myth?*.[17] Travellers invited 'for dinner' with giants discover that they have come not to eat but to be eaten.[18] Lewis' most comic illustration of our capacity for delusion is the Dufflepuds' ignorance about themselves and the Magician, and their ability to contradict themselves without noticing.[19] His most poignant treatment of the power and necessity of unknowing is the stoic resistance of Puddleglum the Marshwiggle to the spells of the Serpent-Witch, when in desperation he stamps barefooted in her fire:

> 'One word, Ma'am,' he said, coming back from the fire; limping because of the pain. 'One word. All you've been saying is quite right, I shouldn't wonder . . . Suppose we *have* only dreamed, or made up, all those things – trees and grass and sun and moon and stars and Aslan himself . . . We're just babies making up a game, if you're right. But four babies playing a game can make a play-world which licks your real world hollow. That's why I'm going to stand by the play-world. I'm on Aslan's side even if there isn't any Aslan to lead it. I'm going to live as like a Narnian as I can even if there isn't any Narnia. So, thanking you kindly for our supper . . . we're leaving your court at once and setting out in the dark to spend our lives looking for the Overland.'[20]

The spell is broken: the Green Witch's true identity is revealed. A Marshwiggle has put into words and deeds of sublime courage the core motif of Dionysius' ascent through negations, and St John's *Ascent of Mount Carmel*: 'setting out in the dark . . . to spend our lives looking'.

The Narnia Chronicles demonstrate the power of stories: stories as anchors we hold on to for dear life when everything else is taken from us, or stories as snares that weaken us and make us captive to ghastly powers.[21] These are stories about what is really good and true, about who really rules and, most importantly of all, about who we are and what we are called to be. Eustace's diary, kept aboard *The Dawn Treader*, is another gently comic gem, laying bare his petty self-deceptions – it's easy to imagine that there is a little of Lewis' autobiography in it.[22] Edmund's treachery is bound up with his fantasy of being greater than his siblings.[23] The destruction of Narnia begins with an ape masquerading as a man, the 'mouthpiece of Aslan'. This brings us to Lewis' use of the apophatic theme of stripping: we need to think of fur coats, snow, a donkey in a lion's skin and a boy in a dragon's.

Paradoxically, the most important point about the fur coats when the Pevensey children arrive in Narnia is not stripping them off but putting them on. They protect the children from the bitter cold and immediately reveal something of the children's truer identity that will only gradually emerge: 'they looked more like royal robes than coats'.[24] Indeed, the first instance of going out in Narnia without such a coat is Edmund's defection to the White Witch. But the coats come from the wardrobe, where there are row upon row of them, other creatures' skins, from which the children choose ones to serve their purpose for a time; they simply jettison them once Narnia begins to thaw.

The fur coat worn by the usurper Queen Jadis is an entirely different matter. When first seen she 'was covered in white fur up to her throat . . . Her face was white – not merely pale, but white like snow or paper or icing-sugar . . .', and at her command the entire land is permanently covered in snow. On his way to find the White Queen, having left behind the fur coat from the wardrobe, Edmund becomes coated instead with snow. It is as if Jadis has thrown her own coat over everything; it freezes, hides the differences between things, erases tracks, prevents growth. Under Jadis' coat it is 'always winter and never Christmas'. Once Aslan has freed the land the only fur coats that will be needed are living skins of badgers and other animals; all dead skins will be laid aside.

Shift the ape persuades Puzzle the donkey to wear a lion-skin and pretend to be Aslan. But a donkey, of course, is not the right shape for a lion-skin, so some alterations are needed: the body needs shortening, the neck lengthening. Even so the charade is pretty unconvincing:

> But if someone who had never seen a lion had looked at Puzzle in his lion-skin he might just mistake him for a lion, if he didn't come too close, and if the light was not too good, and if Puzzle didn't let out a bray and didn't make any noise with his hoofs.[25]

The whole masquerade has to be very carefully managed; that it succeeds at all is a sad illustration of creaturely gullibility and the power of a Great Lie. But just as Jadis in her time of power was not exactly joyful, so Puzzle the donkey becomes increasingly fed-up with the confinement that wearing the lion-skin requires. He is not able to behave like a donkey, by braying, for example; the skin becomes 'increasingly untidy'. In the end, 'Puzzle begged very hard to have the lion-skin taken off him. He said it was too hot and the way it was rucked up on his back was uncomfortable: also, it made him look so silly.'[26]

As Lewis often emphasized, the Narnia stories are not allegories but 'supposals'. He is not doing anything as heavy-handed as *telling* us that people do not only cling to things that are less than the One, but that they even sometimes act as if they were the One. He simply offers us a story and invites us to see whether there is any kind of truth in it. Most of us, if we are honest, will recall a time when we caught sight of ourselves as others see us, and saw something awfully like a donkey's nose poking out from a rumpled and ill-fitting lion-face. Puzzle the donkey might seem to be ridiculous but his discomfort and his keenness to be rid of the disguise are nobler and more honest than the behaviour of some others who wear such gear.

All stripping off is a kind of liberation and therefore ultimately joyous. In cases such as Puzzle's, the hated skin comes off painlessly. But Lewis' most detailed presentation of the theme concerns what happens when the skin we wear has come to fit us so closely that neither we nor anyone other than Aslan can disclose the true self it obscures. In such cases the stripping off is painful and becomes *excruciating* before we can be done with it.

Eustace's 'beastly' nature is abundantly clear to everyone else but he only begins to realize it once he has the body to match. The dragon-body is not entirely a curse: the painful pinch of the gold bracelet he had so desired opens Eustace's heart. He exchanges longing for gold for longing for others. He:

> wanted to be friends. He wanted to get back among humans and talk and laugh and share things. He realized that he was a monster . . . He began to see that the others had not really been fiends at all. He began to wonder if he himself had been such a nice person as he had always supposed. He longed for their voices.[27]

When Aslan leads him to a well of bubbling water and tells him to strip before bathing, Eustace sheds his skin, only to find another dragon-skin beneath it, and then another. The false 'self' isn't shed so easily; it has its own depths.

> 'Then the lion said – but I don't know if it spoke – "You will have to let me undress you." I was afraid of his claws, I can tell you, but I was pretty nearly desperate now. So I just lay flat down on my back to let him do it.
>
> 'The very first tear he made was so deep that I thought it had gone right into my heart . . .'
>
> 'Well, he peeled the beastly stuff right off – just as I thought I'd done it myself the other three times, only they hadn't hurt – and there it was, lying on the grass: only ever so much thicker, and darker, and more knobbly-looking than the others had been. And there was I as smooth and soft as a peeled switch and smaller than I had been.'[28]

Lewis' account of 'The Adventures of Eustace' is thrilling storytelling. But to those familiar with the apophatic way, with its analysis of the dynamics of human desire, with the need for the self to become 'smaller' and the terror and beauty of the night when we are stripped of dead and alien skins, it is also a spiritual myth of profound accuracy.

143

Notes

1 The most recent edition of 'The Weight of Glory' is in a collection under this title by published by Collins (London: 2013). The sermon text is easily accessible online; the description of it as 'one of the most important sermons of the twentieth century' comes from https://blogs.thegospelcoalition.org /evangelical-history/2016/06/08/75-years-ago-today-c-s-lewis-delivers-a-sermon -on-the-weight-of-glory. The title was drawn from 2 Corinthians 4.17: 'For this light momentary affliction is preparing for us an eternal weight of glory beyond all comparison'. Lewis' text for the sermon was Revelation 2.26, 28: 'The one who conquers and who keeps my works until the end, to him I will give authority over the nations . . . And I will give him the morning star.'

2 Lewis even wrote a poem 'On a Theme from Nicholas of Cusa', inspired by Nicholas' *On Learned Ignorance* III.9 – the text is available online at http://poetry nook.com/poem/theme-nicolas-cusa. However, David Downing argues that Lewis was careful to balance apophatic with kataphatic mysticism, and 'emphatically disagreed' with Eckhart's more unbridled apophatic statements – David Downing, *Into the Region of Awe: Mysticism in C. S. Lewis* (Downers Grove, IL: InterVarsity Press, 2005), p. 161.

3 Merton's key works were published from 1948 onwards; we know that Lewis particularly enjoyed his *No Man is an Island* (1955). For such a voracious reader as Lewis it is unlikely he did not explore other works by Merton.

4 *The Voyage of the Dawn Treader* (London: Geoffrey Bles, 1952), ch. 1.

5 Alister McGrath, *The Intellectual World of C. S. Lewis* (Chichester: Wiley-Blackwell, 2014), p. 114.

6 *The Lion, the Witch and the Wardrobe* (London: Geoffrey Bles, 1950), chs 3—9.

7 *The Silver Chair* (London: Geoffrey Bles, 1953), ch. 4; *The Voyage of the Dawn Treader*, chs 7, 10.

8 *The Last Battle* (London: Bodley Head, 1956), ch. 15.

9 *The Lion, the Witch and the Wardrobe*, ch. 17.

10 *The Voyage of the Dawn Treader*, ch. 13. Lewis clearly refers to the Song of Songs in his earlier work of fiction, *The Great Divorce*: 'Hitherto you have experienced truth only with the abstract intellect. I will bring you where you can taste it like honey and be embraced by it as by a bridegroom. Your thirst shall be quenched' (p. 41); cited in McGrath, p. 74. 'The Weight of Glory' also reminds us that we betray our secret longing 'like lovers at the mention of a name'.

11 *The Silver Chair*, ch. 16; Rowan Williams, *The Lion's World: A Journey into the Heart of Narnia* (London: SPCK, 2012), p. 57.

12 *Prince Caspian* (London: Geoffrey Bles, 1951), ch. 10.

13 Ibid.

14 *The Last Battle*, ch. 16.

15 *The Voyage of the Dawn Treader*, ch. 7. Kallistos Ware, 'C. S. Lewis: An "Anonymous orthodox"?', in Judith Wolfe (ed.), *C. S. Lewis and the Church: Essays in Honour of Walter Hooper* (Edinburgh: T. & T. Clark, 2011), pp. 140–4.

16 *The Horse and His Boy* (London: Geoffrey Bles, 1954), ch. 11. Rowan Williams notes that Lewis subsequently commented on the Trinitarian nature of Aslan's statement; Williams, p. 5. There are also interesting echoes in Lewis' slightly

later account of his conversion: in *Surprised by Joy*, published in 1955, there is a threefold recital of the divine identity: 'I am the Lord'; 'I am that I am'; 'I am', followed by the image of God as a stalking cat (pp. 181–2). In chapter 2 of *The Silver Chair*, when Jill Pole encounters Aslan face to face and asks him, 'Then you are Somebody, Sir?', he replies 'I am'.

17 *The Lion, the Witch and the Wardrobe*, ch. 2.

18 *The Silver Chair*, chs 8, 9.

19 *The Voyage of the Dawn Treader*, chs 9, 11.

20 *The Silver Chair*, ch. 12.

21 Lewis distinguished between 'fantastic stories' and 'fantasies', corresponding to 'two kinds of longing. The one is an *askesis*, a spiritual exercise, and the other is a disease'; from his essay 'On Three Ways of Writing for Children', cited by Alan Jacobs in *The Cambridge Companion to C. S. Lewis*, ed. Robert MacSwain and Michael Ward (Cambridge: Cambridge University Press, 2010), p. 278. Like Keats – and of course his friend Tolkien – Lewis believed that myths are particularly suitable stories for conveying the deep truths of the human soul.

22 *The Voyage of the Dawn Treader*, chs 2, 5.

23 *The Lion, the Witch and the Wardrobe*, chs 4, 9.

24 *The Lion, the Witch and the Wardrobe*, ch. 6.

25 *The Last Battle*, ch. 1.

26 *The Last Battle*, ch. 8.

27 *The Voyage of the Dawn Treader*, ch. 6.

28 *The Voyage of the Dawn Treader*, ch. 7.

Zen's 'Don't-Know Mind'

There is a group of people who are committed to living by the principle of not-knowing, taking it as the primary guide for their attitudes and actions. They go by the name of Zen Peacemakers. For them, not-knowing is a discipline of letting go of fixed ideas about themselves, other people and the world; of carefully casting aside biases and assumptions, as fully as possible; and of developing the self-awareness to see where they fail to do this, and address it. It means approaching every situation with an open mind and generous heart.

The Zen Peacemaker Order was founded in the mid-1990s by the New York-based Zen Buddhist teacher Bernie Glassman, and now has members in twelve countries across five continents. Members of the order commit to living by three tenets: not-knowing; bearing witness; taking action. The last two are not so much additions to the first as names for what flows from it. Through their practice of not-knowing they aim to encounter situations directly, without the distorting effect that our perspectives and desires usually have, and thus to bear witness to what is really happening. By means of clear seeing, freed from habitual patterns of emotional or intellectual response, they are enabled to take compassionate and effective action. Both individually and as an order, Zen Peacemakers are involved in training peacemakers, supporting nonviolent activists in conflict zones, and social-action programmes such as prison chaplaincies, educational and medical work.

Roughly a millennium-and-a-half before Glassman, according to legend another Buddhist teacher founded Zen Buddhism itself.

Master Bodhidharma, the story goes, was an Indian monk who came as a missionary to China in the sixth century. By this time some Buddhist ideas and practices had already been transmitted to China via the Silk Road, and Emperor Wu of Liang, in the south-easternmost part of China, was a devoted follower of the Buddha and generous patron of Buddhist monastics and teachers. When the new missionary arrived, the Emperor lost no time in inviting him to his court. The story of what followed – not so much a conversation as an impasse – is one of the founding stories of Zen (or as it is known in China, *Ch'an*). The emperor indicated that he had endowed many monasteries and given other kinds of support to the Dharma, the Buddha's teaching. He enquired: 'How much merit have I accrued?' (In traditional Buddhist teaching, the acquisition of merit, or 'good karma', through virtuous action enables a fortunate rebirth – perhaps as a great king or a heavenly being, or even eventually as a Buddha.) Bodhidharma's reply astonished him: 'None whatsoever.' Taken aback, the emperor demanded to know what new teaching this stranger was expounding, which denied all he had previously understood. 'What', he asked, 'is the fundamental principle of Buddhism?' Bodhidharma replied: 'Vast emptiness, with nothing holy in it.' Even more at a loss, the emperor tried one last time to get to the bottom of it all: 'Who *are* you (to teach this)?' Bodhidharma's answer was immediate and final: 'I don't know.'

According to the official lineage, there are 51 generations of teachers joining Master Bodhidharma and Bernie Glassman in an unbroken line.[1] All of them have taught and handed on the Zen teaching of *mu-shin*: not-knowing, no-mind, don't-know mind.

If you ask the question 'What is wrong with knowing?', Zen has a clear answer: intellectual knowing distorts reality and imprisons us in delusion. Language and thought are dualistic: they separate things out into opposites; *this* and *that* – light and dark, male and female, earth and heaven, love and hate. Reality itself can't be cut up this way. Together with this process of separation, attachment and aversion arise: we love chalk and hate cheese; we belong to one tribe and not another. This way of thinking and being creates a veil of perception-and-projection that overlies the world, separating us from one another, from reality and from our true selves. Zen thus treats knowing as a form of prejudice – literally, *pre-judging* situations, assuming that they conform to categories and principles already fixed in our minds, instead of bringing an open and attentive mind to each new situation as it arises. This analysis is clearly laid out in the early poem 'Engraving Trust in the Heart', attributed to Master Bodhidharma's third-generation heir, known in Japan as Master Sosan. It begins:

> The utmost way is not difficult.
> Just be free of preferences.
> Without attachment or aversion,
> all becomes transparent.
> Missing the way by a hairbreadth,
> you separate earth from sky.
> If you want to see the way as it is,
> do not affirm or deny it.
> Dividing things by opposites
> is a disease of the mind.
> By not seeing the subtle essence,
> you lose your serenity.
> The circle of the way is boundless space.
> There is nothing lacking, nothing extra.
> Grasping and discarding
> will not bring you there.[2]

Zen or *Ch'an* developed in the Far East, out of a movement that began in India, the Mahayana or 'Great Vehicle'. Perhaps the most distinctive teaching of Mahayana Buddhism is *Sunyata*, which is the 'Vast Emptiness' referred to by Master Bodhidharma, and the 'boundless space' of Master Sosan. It is expounded in a set of texts known collectively as the 'Great Perfection of Wisdom Sutras', and boiled down to its most concentrated form in the brief Heart Sutra, which is recited daily in most Zen monasteries and practice centres. According to the Heart Sutra, it is the practice of Wisdom, *Prajna*, that enables us to 'completely relieve misfortune and pain' and achieve the full and perfect freedom and enlightenment known as Nirvana.

Prajna wisdom is not the wisdom of knowing a lot of information and what to do with it. Zen teachers speak of it as a kind of intuition, a wisdom that precedes or transcends the reasoning mind. It is nothing to do with intellect or opinion; in fact these are generally regarded as the most powerful distractions from *prajna*. In order to attain *prajna* wisdom, the masters say, we must 'cast off body and mind'; that is, let go of knowledge, of feelings and emotions, of an identity that defines and delimits. In that empty state we can encounter reality directly, with no distorting agenda, and respond with selfless compassion. This is what the Zen Peacemakers mean by 'not-knowing; bearing witness; taking action'. The text of the Heart Sutra consists of a bravura performance of casting off of the body and mind of Buddhism: one by one it takes all the core teachings of the Buddha, pronounces them empty and notes that in emptiness none of them can be found. Nothing is spared. In emptiness, the sutra declares, there is not even wisdom.

The mind that manifests *prajna* wisdom, therefore, is described as *mu-shin*: no mind, or emptiness-mind. Zen teachers play endless variations on the theme as they seek to help students see: it is 'big mind', 'unborn mind', 'beginner's mind', 'universal mind', 'original mind', 'Big Sky Mind', 'Buddha-mind'. An early seventeenth-century master, Takuan Soho, put it like this:

> The mind of No-mind . . . is by nature never fixed on anything. It is the mind when it has no distinctions, or thoughts, or anything in it. The mind that spreads throughout the mind and permeates the whole is called No-mind. It is the mind that has no abode. We call that which, unlike a stone or tree, has no place to stay, No-mind. If it stops somewhere, there is something in the mind, but if it has no stopping-place, there is nothing in the mind. We call having nothing in the mind, the mind of No-mind, or No-mind, No-thought.[3]

One of the classic texts of English-language Zen is *Zen Mind, Beginner's Mind* by the Japanese master Shunryu Suzuki, published in 1970. Suzuki's successor Richard Baker supplied an explanatory introduction:

> The practice of Zen mind is beginner's mind. The innocence of the first enquiry – what am I? – is needed throughout Zen practice. The mind of the beginner is empty, free of the habits of the expert, ready to accept, to doubt, and open to all the possibilities. It is the kind of mind which can see things as they are.[4]

Only a mind – such as Bodhidharma's – that does not already know its identity is able to make that 'first enquiry' in a state of innocence.

Despite Takuan Soho's words about 'having nothing in the mind', Zen's no-mind is not blank vacancy or placid ignorance; the Zen Peacemakers describe it as 'open presence without separation', receptive, welcoming, attentive. These are, of course, characteristics of a whole person, not just of a disembodied and uncontextualized mind. To achieve and maintain such a state requires discipline and practice; therefore Zen has developed a range of techniques to aid the student, including its well-known association with archery and other martial arts, with calligraphy, poetry and the tea ceremony (though unfortunately not traditionally with motorcycle maintenance). One of the most focused and distinctive Zen techniques is the practice of *koan* study.

Zen *koans* are taken from stories of conversations between Zen practitioners. The *koan* may be a whole story or a simple phrase (often a question), even a single word. Some have become well known outside Zen circles, such as the question: 'What is the sound of one hand clapping?'

Koans are used in a variety of ways by different teachers; in its most complex form, *koan* study is a curriculum of a few hundred *koans*, grouped into discrete stages to help a student throw off the habits of discriminative or rationalistic thought, and to develop a thorough awakening to the reality that lies beyond all words and thoughts – a reality variously described as the true or original self, as Buddha-nature, enlightenment or Suchness. There are several published collections of *koans*, some with commentaries attached; the best known is the *Mumonkan*, a compilation of 49 *koans* made by the thirteenth-century Chinese Master Mumon Ekai. (The story of Master Bodhidharma's meeting with Emperor Lu is the first in an earlier collection of one hundred *koans*, the *Hekiganroku* or 'Blue Cliff Records'.)

Many of the *koans* in the *Mumonkan* collection report conversations about Zen mind. Case 19 recalls a conversation between the Chinese Master Nansen and his disciple Joshu, who later became a much-loved Master:

> Joshu asked Nansen, 'What is the Way?' 'Ordinary mind is the Way,' Nansen replied. 'Shall I try to seek after it?' Joshu asked. 'If you try for it, you will become separated from it,' responded Nansen. 'How can I know the Way unless I try for it?' persisted Joshu. Nansen said, '. . . When you have really reached the true Way beyond doubt, you will find it as vast and boundless as outer space. How can it be talked about on the level of right and wrong?' With these words, Joshu came to a sudden realization.[5]

In his commentary on this case, Katsuki Sekida explains ordinary mind as the mind that children, animals, plants and minerals have. Human adults have it too, when we are absorbed in an activity like gardening or dancing: we are attentive, focused and completely without self-consciousness or dualistic thought. This is what Billy Elliot meant in Lee Hall's screenplay for the 2000 film, when asked what it felt like when he danced: 'Don't know. Sorta feels good. Sorta stiff and that, but once I get going . . . then I like, forget everything. And . . . sorta disappear. Sorta disappear.'[62] Of course, thinking about ordinary mind as a goal and trying to achieve it will be absolutely self-defeating: if we try for it, we will be forever separated from it. Joshu came to a sudden realization not because he worked this out logically but because Nansen's apophatic words struck him as a hammer strikes a gong.

In 1965 Pope Paul VI approved release of *Nostra Aetate*, a 'Declaration on the Relation of the Church with Non-Christian

Religions', in the aftermath of the Second Vatican Council. In the words of the Jesuit priest Robert Kennedy, the Declaration:

> explains that the Catholic religion rejects nothing of all that which is true and holy in these [non-Christian] religions. Not only does the Church not reject what is true and holy in non-Christian religions, but it encourages us to seek out positively and accept whatever they possess that is true and holy.[7]

Kennedy and an increasing number of other pioneers attest to finding something 'true and holy' in Zen's practice of don't-know mind. For Kennedy, 'it can deepen Christian prayer and root our faith not just in our head but in our whole person.'[8] The English Benedictine Tom Chetwynd argued that Zen preserves in a living tradition the contemplative prayer-practice of Jesus himself, practised and taught for centuries within the Church but sadly hardly any longer in mainstream Western Christianity; for Chetwynd, Zen is not only a delightfully lively ally on the journey but offers a kind of fostering service for Christians who have lost touch with their home tradition of contemplative prayer.[9]

Zen isn't alone: there are apophatic traditions in Sufism, Hinduism, Judaism and elsewhere. Christians may from time to time gain instruction or succour by accepting the gracious hospitality of those who teach and practise in these other faiths. This is not to say that Zen's don't-know mind or emptiness mind is the same thing as Meister Eckhart's detached mind 'free from prayer' or Nicholas of Cusa's 'learned ignorance', or that all these faith traditions are 'basically the same'. That would be a crass pre-judgement. Nor is it to say that everything in these faiths is true and holy; nor that any alliance with them need be all-encompassing and for ever. Kennedy, Chetwynd and others simply give their testimony to the possibility that Zen can help us with the business of stripping off until we are naked in the presence of our God.

We have noticed repeatedly already how words get in our way, trip us up, separate us from reality, and in particular how much of the problem springs from their dualistic character. We have noticed also the irony that we still need to use words to make this point; so that the apophatic traditions all resort to abusing language, twisting, distorting even breaking it. By now, therefore, there will be no surprise in discovering that Zen both utilizes the distinction between knowing and not-knowing and resists it. Some words were missing from Nansen's reply to Joshu quoted above. Nansen's full reply, in Sekida's translation, was as follows:

> The Way is not a matter of knowing or not knowing. Knowing is delusion; not knowing is confusion. When you have really reached the true Way beyond doubt, you will find it as vast and boundless as outer space. How can it be talked about on the level of right and wrong?

By 'not knowing' in this *koan*, Nansen means the ignorance of confusion, which is the opposite of 'knowing' and is as different from the practice of don't-know mind as brute ignorance is from learned ignorance. To put it another way, not-knowing can *either* mean the state of ignorance that is the contradictory of knowing, *or* it can refer apophatically to an active stripping off of knowledge. The words themselves won't help you work out which is which; that is the work of *prajna* wisdom.

Not all Zen teachers and students use *koan* training. The main alternative is the tradition of 'just sitting' or 'simply sitting' (in Japanese, *shikantaza*), whose most influential champion is the thirteenth-century Japanese Master Dogen. Dogen saw clearly that, in a practice devoted to returning to a mind of non-separation, the separation between thinking and non-thinking, like that between knowing and not-knowing, can be misleading. He therefore introduces a third term to capture more closely the significance of Zen's don't-know mind, and the essential practice of 'simply sitting':

> After Great Master Yakusan Kodo had finished a period of zazen [seated meditation] a monk asked, 'What do you think about

as you sit so intensely?' The Master said, 'I think not-thinking.' The monk asked, 'How can you think not-thinking?' The Master replied, 'Non-thinking.'[10]

Non-thinking is not the opposite of thinking or of not-thinking. It is something altogether different – a state *beyond* thinking, or a mind *other than* thinking. Once again, the best way to understand what this means, Dogen suggests, is simply to notice it happening in our own experience – as Billy Elliot did. Sitting and paying attention is one way to do this. Dancing often helps.

Notes

1 This is the lineage of the White Plum Asangha, a worldwide network of teachers descended from Glassman's own teacher, Taezan Maezumi.

2 Kazuaki Tanahashi, *Zen Chants: Thirty-Five Essential Texts with Commentary* (Boston: Shambala, 2015), p. 67. Other translations of the text are readily available online.

3 Takuan Soho, *Fudochi Shinmyoroku* [Admirable Records of Unmoving Wisdom], cited by J. Kakichi Kadowaki, translated by Joan Rieck, in *Zen and the Bible* (Maryknoll, NY: Orbis, 2002), p. 77.

4 Richard Baker, in Shunryu Suzuki, *Zen Mind, Beginner's Mind* (New York: Weatherhill, 1970), pp. 13–14.

5 Katsuki Sekida's translation in *Two Zen Classics: Mumonkan and Hekiganroku* (New York: Weatherhill, 1977), pp. 73–5.

6 *Billy Elliot*, 2000, BBC Films/Tiger Aspect Pictures/Working Title.

7 Robert E. Kennedy, *Zen Spirit, Christian Spirit: The Place of Zen in Christian Life* (New York: Continuum, 2007), p. 17.

8 Ibid.

9 Tom Chetwynd, *Zen and the Kingdom of Heaven: Reflections on the Tradition of Meditation in Christianity and Zen Buddhism* (Boston: Wisdom, 2001).

10 Master Dogen, *Shobogenzo Zazenshin*, translated by Kosen Nishiyama et al. (Tokyo: Nakayama Shobo, 1983), Vol. 4, p. 47. The text is also available online in other translations.

PART 5

Apophatic Practices

Carole Bury, 'Your Very Bones will Vibrate with Life'.

Exuberance: Saying and Unsaying in Parable and Poetry

In my village church – as in most churches built before the twenti-eth century – between the high altar and the nave there lies a space just big enough to dance in. Its boundaries are marked to the west by pulpit and lectern and to the east by an altar rail. In grander churches the frontier materializes as a rood screen. In-between the mundane prose of the pews (where we chatter with one another about family events and neighbourhood news; where the words of, to and from God compete for space among a conversational crowd) and the near silence of the sanctuary (where the Word breaks like waves on a further shore) – in this arena words take flight and soar among angels. In the choir, prose gives way to chant, metre, song, psalm and hymn.

Perhaps we began this account of apophasis in the wrong place.

We began by noticing the inadequacy of words to grasp what is beyond duality. Now, as we approach the altar, we begin to see words transfigured, indwelt by spirit. Words are no longer primar-ily used to speak *of* God; 'Thou' replaces 'He'. As lovers, we sing to God; the meaning of our songs is in the delight or longing or lament they convey, not in the sense of the words but beyond them, in what, like birds, they fly towards.

If we had begun instead at the right end we might have noticed that when God speaks, a cosmos tumbles into being. Divine words are not words in our sense at all but worlds and souls, beings and becomings. God's speech is poetic – literally: *poiesis* is the Greek for 'creation', 'creativity'. Angels and all creation are thought, in the Bible, to sing endless praises. This is what speech is for, primarily. 'Orthodoxy' is only secondarily 'right belief'; its greater meaning is 'right praise' – as in the 'doxology'. The words of every day are mere shadows and simulacra of holy originals.

Plato, we noticed, thought that in order to penetrate appearance and opinion, and to apprehend reality, the kind of (un)learning we need to do is a stripping back, a recourse to faculties of memory and imagination, and that this process demands personal commitment. There is the commitment of desire, or longing: he gets a few cheap laughs with an analogy between the philosopher and the promiscuous lover. There is the commitment of conversational engagement, in the process of 'dialectic'. There is the commitment of the intellect, which through the symbolic language of geometry and mathematics will uncover the deep structures of the world – as Galileo did, and Einstein. There is the commitment of the self: it is deep in the recesses of the memory, of the heart, that the 'ideal forms' will be unearthed. The types of speech that will engage us in these processes of committed enquiry are rarely prosaic. Socrates was believed to imperil the safety of Athens *simply by talking* (we are also told about his characteristic – and equally infuriating – silences). Plato's Socrates is distinguished not so much by what he says as by what he *asks* – it is his questions, and their results in hearts and lives, not his claims, that disrupt good order. Further, as we saw earlier, when he turns to speak of the ultimate, he takes refuge in metaphor, simile, analogy and myth. In such forms of discourse, meaning emerges both in a complex interplay between speakers, dependent on the particular skills, experiences and purposes they bring, and in the relationships between different situations, as a delicate web that flexes into each new occasion. This is a form of meaning without closure, where conclusions are only ever tentative and partial and statements are always invitations to respond.

Speech of such a kind is no longer antithetical to silence; it requires silence in which to reverberate, just as a bell must be hollow in order to ring. Like a struck bell too, the purpose and effect of such speech is not simply to open our senses and minds to a reality independent of us but to change us, bringing us into new relation with reality. Maggie Ross makes just this point:

the gifts from deep mind and the process of exchange are holistic and require a multivalent, resonant language – hence the need for metaphor, poetry, and mythology. The tendency of ancient, late antique, and medieval writers to resort to story, myth, and metaphor are designed to engage the imagination, to move readers into liminality, to open them to the resonance of the deep mind, to stimulate the desire to persevere – all of which enrich and deepen engagement with the deep mind and its context of silence and the capacity to receive its gifts.[1]

The Bible is the sourcebook of Christian theology: *theou-logos*, the record of God's creative words, words about the Word, divine words issuing forth from silence, human words echoing towards silence. It is a book of stories, where histories become myths by bearing the burden of a truth beyond themselves, a book of song and poem, paradox and proverb, conversation, claim and counter-claim. Almost everything the Bible says about God it also somewhere unsays. At its apophatic heart we find Moses, John and Jesus.

In the Song of Songs we saw how the mutual delight of lover and beloved piles up words and images with giddy exuberance, in what Francis Landy called 'verbal magic'. The magic lies in the interaction between words and audience: the accretion of words does not serve a steady accumulation of meaning but creates a jostling and unsettled space; vertiginous excess of words topples us into the space of mystery. Like a riddle or a Zen *koan*, the question they pose is 'What?'

In kataphatic theology, words have an order: words fit things. The correct word for the thing by my right hand at the moment is 'coffee'. The closest-fitting word for the Absolute Beyond is 'God'. Other words can then be ranked against these: 'spirit' and 'good' are much nearer 'God' than are 'gum' or 'twisted'. Apophatic theology overturns this hierarchical order with a free-for-all between all words and none. We have heard already Dionysius' preference for 'unlike likenesses', his performance of the ascent to silence, intertwined with a virtually untranslatable fecundity of words. It is as if the beyond upsets our stomachs, leading either to a blockage of speech or an explosive logorrhoea:

When we attempt to speak of God one of two possibilities occurs. Either our speech is blown apart by the immensity of God or we are struck dumb because we cannot speak of that which is God. Either we cannot stop speaking or we can say nothing at all. We either have to use every metaphor that is to hand or no metaphors at all. The only two possibilities for those who wish to speak about God are either too much speech or no speech at all. This is the source of all that the Church has called mysticism.[2]

Many modern writers on Christian mysticism have commented on this apophatic promiscuity of words: the quotation above is from Melvyn Matthews. The 'either/or' here is not quite the disjunction it seems: as in Dionysius, the logorrhoea itself underscores and points us back to the dumbness. Thomas Merton makes the same point, joining the dots to the aesthetic and sacramental arts: all things and all concepts are capable of becoming valid signs of divinity, if our gaze penetrates through them to the beyond.[3] C. S. Lewis likewise noted that in 'commerce with . . . the naked [imageless] Other . . . our imagination salutes it with a hundred images'.[4] Martin Laird, drawing on Gregory of Nyssa's commentary on the Song of Songs, coined the word 'logophasis' to signify the words that pour out of those who have followed the apophatic path to union with the Word: these are words from a divine source, an ever-flowing stream;[5] words that salute the holy, greet it, acknowledge its claim on our attention, address it; words that embody it.

Poetry, then.

'Poetry puts language in a state of emergency', says Mark Oakley,[6] a state of emergency where normal laws are suspended, people are displaced, life is lived in the light of the unexpected, the status quo is profoundly at risk. Poets confess that their poems take them by surprise, flow from heaven knows where, say more than their authors intend or understand. Readers and hearers confess that poems disrupt order, intend and attend detonations, collisions and inundations, save lives. Keats dismisses safe poems, words that refuse to surrender control, as the 'wordsworthian or egotistical sublime'; the negative capability of true poetry is what enables the soul, like Apollo, to 'die into life'.

Poetry is one of the languages of apophasis/logophasis. Poetry and song celebrate the material aspects of speech, the incarnational roots of our words: in rhythm and rhyme, assonance and alliteration, the flesh of lip and tongue, the architecture of vocal cords and the resonance of chambers of speech, the vibrations of tympanum, hammer and anvil, the reverberations of cochlear chambers – all of these root and channel meaning in and through bodies, anchor it in bone and membrane, requiring moisture and shape, endowing speech with particularities of place and tone, aligning or syncopating with the body's own rhythms of breath and pulse. Poems speak with, as Oakley says, 'the more human voice'.[7]

Poems address mystery and reality sufficiently obliquely that in them we can, as Emily Dickinson demanded, 'tell the truth [a]slant'. A sacramental, 'slant' approach to truth is used in Judith Wright's poem 'Grace'. Reality is sliced open in such a way as to reveal a greater surface area than the direct cut of declarative speech, making it clear that how you see this thing depends on which direction you look at it from, indirectly but insistently suggesting that you might consider shifting your stance.

> Living is dailiness, a simple bread
> that's worth the eating. But I have known a wine,
> a drunkenness that can't be spoke or sung
> without betraying it. Far past Yours or Mine,
> even past Ours, it has nothing at all to say;
> it slants a sudden laser through common day.[8]

Even further: poems are capable of creating both a space for personal growth and a shape to form us within it. This is Coleridge's insight, which he names the 'sacred power of self-intuition':

> They and they only can acquire the philosophic imagination, the sacred power of self-intuition, who within themselves can interpret and understand the symbol, that the wings of the air-sylph are forming within the skin of the caterpillar; those only, who feel in their own spirits the same instinct, which impels the

chrysalis of the horned fly to leave the room in its involucrum for antennae yet to come. They know and feel, that the potential works in them, even as the actual works on them.[9]

Poems are sculptures made of words. In sculptures there are two kinds of significant space. There is the absence of material that has been chipped, filed or pinched away in order to allow form to emerge. And then there is the space incorporated within the statue itself. These significant spaces are often called 'negative space'. The negative space in a poem lies in-between the words. Coleridge's image of transformation resonates with Anna Kamienska's poem of the same name, cited by Robin Meyers to illustrate the necessity of our own undoing, our 'tumbling from the saddle of illusion'. In this process, Kamienska avers, you must 'thread yourself through yourself . . . so that each word runs to the other side of truth'.[10]

The Bible is full of poems. Much more of it is formally poetry, or even hymn, than is apparent at first glance. Consider, for example, the 'Hymn to the Cosmic Christ' in Colossians 1.15–20, or these cold lines of despair from the otherwise savagely comic book of Jonah (2.5–6):

> The waters closed in over me to take my life;
>   the deep surrounded me;
> weeds were wrapped around my head
>   at the roots of the mountains.

Like germs of both kinds – seeds and infections – poems and songs do not sit still in their assigned places within the biblical text but invade their host. In the end there appears to be no safe ground where we can lay aside our poetic sensibilities and read the text straight up and down. Thus words on paper become sacraments, carriers of the wild uncontainable energies of grace, broken to cleanse and feed us, splashed and consumed to restore us to life.

Poetry's creeping infection of apparently prosaic speech leaves detectable traces, among them metaphor and simile, exaggeration, parable, narrative and, most particularly, paradox. Paradox pervades apophatic spirituality: it governs the biblical images of the bush that burns without being consumed and of the lover who runs all the way from the mountain grazing-fields to search out the door of his beloved but does not linger long enough to be admitted. It is the watermark of the Nicene Creed, affirming both the full divinity and the full humanity of Jesus Christ, and of the later Chalcedonian Definition of faith, ruling out both separation and combination of those two natures. We have encountered it in St John of the Cross's *todo y nada*, all and nothing, and in Nicholas of Cusa's 'learned ignorance' and 'otherness without otherness'. Catherine Keller makes the link between Nicholas' 'Possibility Itself' and the words of Emily Dickinson, America's beloved apophatic poet:

I dwell in Possibility –
A fairer House than Prose –
More numerous of Windows –
Superior – for Doors – [11]

Thomas Merton describes our journey towards holy encounter with a typical paradox: 'God approaches our minds by receding from them ... We know Him better after our minds have let Him go.'[12]

Jesus' teachings, according to the Gospel record, are full of paradox. 'Whoever who finds his life will lose it' (Matthew 10.39); 'The greatest among you shall be your servant' (Matthew 23.11); 'Blessed are you when others revile you and persecute you' (Matthew 5.11). He taught in homely parables, we are instructed, not to help people understand but so that they would not (Mark 4.10–12). The verbal paradoxes are the least of it: his actions are even more thoroughly imbued with paradox, such as the 'triumphal entry' into Jerusalem riding not a majestic warhorse but an *ass* (Matthew 21.1–9); the cursing of a fig tree for not bearing figs *when it was not the season for figs* (Mark 11.13); and his washing his disciples' feet (John 13.3–5) – an action offensive enough by the standards of the day but made pointless in practical terms by being done *during* rather than before supper. In our day this sort of behaviour belongs properly to clowns.

The apophatic theologian insists that these paradoxes go all the way to the end; they are not resolved. The cross is never uncrossed. We recall that Nicholas' 'coincidence of opposites' is a tangled heap not straightened out but breached, in union with God. Remarkably, scientists are now theology's best collaborators in this matter: as Maggie Ross explains, the 'accuracy and rigour of paradox as descriptor' is a corollary of a post-Einsteinian view of cosmic reality, involving a:

> shift from a photographic to a holographic perspective, from a two or three dimensional mechanical universe, where cause, effect, and entropy reign supreme and can be analysed systematically by a mythical objective observer using a 'cartesian grid', to a multidimensional universe – twenty-two dimensions according to one version of super-string theory – a universe that is contingent, chaotic, relational and interactive, where all time exists in every moment, and motion and all space exists at each point of time, where particles are said to make decisions, quarks and forces are spoken of in terms of flavours and colours, and indeterminacy is the rule of order; where paradox is the normal descriptor, the observer is part of what is observed, and the whole is an 'implicate order', to use David Bohm's phrase . . .[13]

Some philosophers and mathematicians, therefore, are now beginning to work with *paraconsistent* logic, and under the rubric of *dialetheism* – which, paradoxically, is nothing to do with religious 'theism' but derives its name from the Greek word for truth, *aletheia* (*dy-aletheia*: 'two truths'). They are acknowledging that if the fundamental nature of the universe is really such as it now appears to be, our definitions of truth and logic need to incorporate difference and contradiction. What we intuit of the Creator turns out not to be so far removed from creation after all – though the love poets have known this immemorially.

For the time being, let us give the last word on poetry and paradox to the beautiful poet of divine love, St John of the Cross, in his Prologue to *The Spiritual Canticle*:

The wisdom and charity of God is so vast ... that it reaches from end to end, and those informed and moved by it bear in some way this very abundance and impulsiveness in their words ...

Who can describe the understanding He gives to loving souls in whom He dwells? And who can express the experience He imparts to them? Who, finally, can explain the desires He gives them? Certainly, no one can! Not even they who receive these communications. As a result these persons let something of their experiences overflow in figures and similes, and from the abundance of their spirit pour out secrets and mysteries rather than rational explanations.[14]

Notes

1 Maggie Ross, Silence: *A User's Guide* (London: Darton, Longman & Todd, 2014), p. 32.

2 Melvyn Matthews, *Both Alike to Thee: The Retrieval of the Mystical Way* (London: SPCK, 2000), pp. 84–5.

3 Thomas Merton, *Contemplative Prayer* (London: Darton, Longman & Todd, 1973), pp. 104–7.

4 C. S. Lewis, *Surprised by Joy*, cited in David Downing, *Into the Region of Awe: Mysticism in C. S. Lewis* (Downers Grove, IL: InterVarsity Press, 2005), p. 110.

5 Martin Laird, *Gregory of Nyssa and the Grasp of Faith: Union, Knowledge and Divine Presence* (Oxford: Oxford University Press, 2004), p. 167.

6 Mark Oakley, *The Splash of Words: Believing in Poetry* (Norwich: Canterbury Press, 2016), p. xvi.

7 Ibid., p. xviii.

8 Judith Wright, *Collected Poems* 1942–85 (Sydney: Angus & Robertson, 1994), pp. 331–2, cited in William Countryman, *The Poetic Imagination: An Anglican Spiritual Tradition* (London: Darton, Longman & Todd, 1999), p. 69.

9 Coleridge, *Biographica Literaria*, Vol. 1, pp. 241–2, cited by Malcolm Guite in *Mariner: A Voyage with Samuel Taylor Coleridge* (London: Hodder & Stoughton, 2017), p. 7.

10 Robin Meyers, *Spiritual Defiance: Building a Beloved Community of Resistance* (New Haven, CT: Yale University Press, 2015), pp. 1–17; Anna Kamienska's poem 'Transformation', cited on pp. 5–6, comes from *Astonishments: Selected Poems of Anna Kamienska*, translation and compilation copyright © 2007 by Grazyna Drabik and David Curzon (Brewster, MA: Paraclete Press, 2011), p. 79. Polish text copyright © 2007 by Pawel Spiewak. Used by permission of Paraclete Press: www.paracletepress.com.

11 Emily Dickinson, 'I dwell in Possibility', in *The Complete Poems of Emily Dickinson*, edited by Thomas H. Johnson (London: Faber & Faber, 1970), p. 327.

12 Thomas Merton, *No Man is an Island* (Tunbridge Wells: Burns & Oates, 1955), p. 210.

13 Maggie Ross, 'Apophatic Prayer as a Theological Model: Seeking Coordinates in the Ineffable Notes for a Quantum Theology', in *Literature and Theology* 7/4, pp. 325–53 (December 1993), p. 325 and n. 3.

14 *The Spiritual Canticle*, quoting Kieran Kavanaugh's translation in *John of the Cross: Selected Writings* for the Classics of Western Spirituality series (New York: Paulist Press, 1987), pp. 219–20.

Pilgrimage

Anyone who prepares to undertake a pilgrimage finds him- or herself very quickly in a practical relationship with those two great Old Testament images of holy encounter: bare feet and stripping off. Stories circulate of blister torments – of blisters upon blisters, of bleeding and infection – and how to avoid them by rubbing the feet regularly with vinegar or alcohol, by using bandages or gel. We peel off our socks and anxiously examine our extremities for signs of potential weakness.

Pilgrims know the paradox of packing: pack too much and you will have to discard some of your kit along the way in order to make the load bearable; yet if you don't bring absolutely everything, the one thing you don't bring will be the exact thing you need. Or like as not, if you did pack it you will mislay, exhaust or break it on the journey. The age-old solution is mutual assistance – in other words, *borrowing*. As you trudge along the path, blisters buffered by someone else's plasters, nose shiny with someone else's sunscreen, you discover that those on the road hold possessions more lightly; that there is joy in giving and receiving good and necessary things.

As pilgrims we are vulnerable. The land we travel through is not our own; we have no claim, no *right* there. The languages we speak may not be spoken there, the codes we live by may not be honoured. We come into places not our own and experience our fragility and dependence on things and beings beyond our control. It isn't just plasters and sunscreen that are shared on the road: we share news with other travellers, we point out to one another resources and shelters.

The road itself will offer us new sights and experiences, but as we exchange stories with other travellers, as they warn us of dangers or advise us of delights, we are exchanging perspectives too – borrowing one another's ways of seeing. So we learn not only that there is more 'out there' than we have seen or known but also that there are more ways of seeing it than we can count. With luck, we begin to see that there is never one vantage point from which one can see all the terrain, but only different perspectives. One very particular type of pilgrimage is circumambulation, the ancient religious practice of walking in a circle around a sacred site. Here in refined form is the same wisdom: always the same goal or focus, but always looking different, according to the pilgrim's standpoint.

At first sight it may seem that a journey of pilgrimage has both a starting point and an end. In experience, neither of these is straightforward.

Sometimes the place we begin from is not – or does not feel like – home; we may be unsure where 'home' really is or whether we have ever really been there. As Augustine said, our hearts have always been restless. With some pilgrimages it is difficult to pinpoint when we really began: we have often been travelling towards the destination or preparing for the journey for a long time before we realize it. And after all that, if we return 'home' we discover that – maybe for better, maybe for worse – it is not quite what we thought it was. We come back changed, and therefore home is no longer what it once was for us. Bilbo and Frodo Baggins have shown us all that much.

The clarity of the destination, too, tends to unravel. We travel with a mental image of the goal – Santiago de Compostela, perhaps. When we arrive at the earthly Santiago it is not as we imagined. Probably it is damper and noisier; for the lucky few, it may surpass expectation. The experience is concrete whereas the expectation – or perhaps the memory – was abstract. The goal we have gained turns out not to be what we thought we sought. Nor do we gain it comprehensively, conclusively: we cannot linger there until the clouds part; we cannot stay long enough to see it all.

Sometimes the destination turns out not to have been the point of the journey at all. People say such things as 'I thought I would arrive and find something of the presence of God, but when I got there I realized I had known his presence all along, at every stage on the path.' Alternatively, we may gain our goal and find that even as we grasp it, it has slipped through our fingers. This is the truth expressed in the Song of Songs and in Gregory of Nyssa's insight that our appetite for the divine grows as it is fed.

Thus even if it appears that we have reached the destination of an earthly pilgrimage, we never completely and finally *arrive*. Our pilgrimage is perpetual. This was beautifully expressed in the practice of the Celtic saints such as Columba, who embarked on a pilgrimage without a destination – they simply clambered into their coracles to be carried by the wind and Spirit, to stay wherever they landed until it was time to move again. It was also expressed in the practice of the class of monks called Gyrovagues – pure itinerants who wandered from monastery to monastery without settling or belonging anywhere other than on the road. In their example we see the transformation of 'journeying': the road is no longer a means to get us somewhere else but a home that is no home. In pilgrimage, our way becomes The Way.

Pilgrimage is above all a discipline of exile. As Frédéric Gros explains:

> The primary meaning of peregrinus is *foreigner* or exile. The pilgrim, originally, is not one who is heading somewhere (Rome, Jerusalem, etc.), but essentially one who *is not at home where he is walking* . . . he's a stranger, a foreigner.[1]

St Paul notes that we are resident aliens on earth: 'our citizenship is in heaven' (Philippians 3.20). There are both practical and theological links back to Jesus, who 'has nowhere to lay his head' (Luke 9.58) and who 'came down from heaven' (John 6.58) and 'dwelt among us' (John 1.14). St Augustine develops the theme in his *City of God* and elsewhere: Christians are 'on pilgrimage from their fatherland'. Thus the path of the pilgrim fuses footwork and soulwork: the exterior path mirrors an inner journey.

Pilgrimage is an extended reversal of 'normality'. As outsiders, pilgrims are displaced from their accustomed privileges: they are often confused with those other 'outsider' groups, vagabonds and tramps, the 'great unwashed', the homeless. Ideally, something of the vagrant perspective rubs off – another way apophatic practice is inseparable from growth in compassion and from action on behalf of others.

> During my pilgrimage through Arizona I was arrested by a plain-clothes policeman . . . After a short ride in a patrol car I was booked as a vagrant. When you walk on faith you are techni-cally guilty of vagrancy. Yes, I've been jailed several times for not having any money . . . They put me into a huge inner room sur-rounded by cell blocks in which they locked me with women, four to a cell for the night. As I walked in I said to myself, 'Peace Pilgrim, you have dedicated your life to service – behold your wonderful new field of service!'[2]

Our settled lives tend to be marked by a series of orderly separations between public and private activities, 'family' and 'others', indoors and outdoors, but on the road that pattern breaks down, as every-one knows who has walked a long route with no toilet provision, or shared a sleeping-platform with a complete stranger. We learn that what might have seemed inappropriate or even intolerable can be managed with dignity and mutual respect.

Boundaries themselves metamorphose. To the pilgrim they are not so much frontiers as assurances of progress, targets to reach and cross. Pilgrims become connoisseurs of different methods of crossing: designs of stile or ford matter because those with different infirmities will find some easier than others. Sooner or later most of us will need to accept help. Ingenuity in overcoming barriers is prized: the pilgrim who helps others across electric fences or deep water is a celebrated hero. Pilgrims can also foment revolution, then, as in Jack Kerouac's famous vision:

> Pain or love or danger makes you real again, ain't that right . . . That's why frontiersmen are always heroes and were always my real heroes and will always be. They're constantly on the alert in the realness which might as well be real as unreal . . . I see a vision of a great rucksack revolution thousands or even millions of young Americans wandering around with rucksacks, going up mountains to pray, making children laugh and old men glad, making young girls happy and old girls happier . . .[3]

Pilgrims are curious, eager for news on the road, accumulating scraps of local lore; gratefully they follow a recommendation to turn aside from the planned route and take in a sublime viewpoint or safe shortcut. Yet no one loves a know-it-all, on the road least of all. The pilgrim's inexpertise is the precondition for discovery and delight. Knowledge and experience are to be worn lightly here.

The pilgrim knows in the body the truth of Alfred Korzybski's celebrated aphorism that 'the map is not the territory': more than one dimension is missing from the page. There is a stretch of the West Highland Way, for instance, when you suddenly seem to be walking on stardust: the quartz in the rock underfoot glints and sparkles. The guidebook *might have* told you that, but not how your eyes would prick with tears for the delight of it, or how hard you'd find it on that diamond-sparkling path not to seize a stranger for an impromptu Fred-and-Ginger song and dance. Scent and colour, the pull of gradient on the muscles of leg and trunk, the accidents of birdcry and cloud formation, are known only to those who have made the journey: 'It was on *that* rock that I slipped and gashed my foot and limped for the next three days . . .' The map tells us only of the path, but in our experience knowing the path is inseparable from knowing ourselves, how we were on the journey and how it marked us.

Instead of journeys as defined periods punctuating a settled life, periods of transition 'there and back again', we are invited to see the whole of life as journey. Jesus proclaims himself the 'only Way' (John 14.6), and his followers are 'Followers of the Way' (a designation shared, incidentally, with Buddhists and Taoists).

Many of the experiences of everyday life assume much greater significance on pilgrimage, simply because of our vulnerability and our distance from the resources of 'home': sharing, for example, and gift. Perhaps foremost is the experience of hospitality: it is one thing to leave home, be welcomed by another and then return home, but to be welcomed into someone else's home while one is – temporarily or permanently – homeless is a different matter entirely. Baths, iced drinks, opportunity for laundry and the bliss of freeing the feet from one's boots – these are delights. We are given time to recover ourselves. The pilgrim receiving hospitality temporarily swaps activity and self-motivation for a disciplined receptivity. It is not always easy: there are still the challenges of local custom, strange foodstuffs, the possibility of unintentional transgression and offence. There is an unspoken rule of reciprocity: the guest brings news, entertains with stories, offers appreciation. Some hosts water their hospitality down with arrogance, power play or insensitivity. The beautiful meeting of minds and hearts can never be taken for granted, but it happens nonetheless with gracious regularity: in the hospitality of the 'other' we find something new and precious, or an unexpected link with the old and familiar. New sympathies and new connections form. What we receive enlarges mind and heart as well as stomach.

Many spiritual traditions remind us that in receiving strangers we sometimes receive 'angels unawares', or even the divine presence. Benedictine monks are enjoined to receive travellers and guests as if they received Christ himself. Jesus assembled and reassembled his followers at meals where he was sometimes host and sometimes guest; he gave a great deal of advice on how to treat guests. Each of us takes our turn as host and guest to others.

The texts and themes of the apophatic tradition may still be largely unknown in our culture, but this practice of pilgrimage is now easily accessible. The recent huge growth in popularity for pilgrimages of all kinds is well documented; it appeals to an age that wants spiritual exploration without the constraints of institutional religion. Local, national and international pilgrimage routes are well publicized and equipped; facilities are available for both solo and group pilgrimages, lasting minutes or months.

Pilgrimage as a spiritual practice is ancient – more ancient than the texts and stories that give us our first glimpses of it. Even to call it 'a spiritual practice' at all is anachronistic: ancient nomads would not have made a distinction between sacred and mundane journeys. Nevertheless, we can see that the mind of the traveller can turn even the most prosaic journey into a pilgrimage of the heart and mind, while even the most 'spiritual' of pilgrimages can be all too easily brought down to the level of chatter and commerce. So it would be preposterous to claim that pilgrimage is unavoidably apophatic. And yet the nature of pilgrimage is such that it can often begin its work in us before we bestow our awareness or consent, as Martin Robinson says: 'Many set off on pilgrimage with little concept of what the interior journey might mean and meet themselves *en route* in surprising and sometimes disturbing ways.'[4]

The practice of pilgrimage is a familiar metaphor for the whole Christian life. In all its reversals, changes of perspective, shedding of layers, shifting of standpoints, valuing of inexperience and its dissolving of boundaries, most especially the distinction between the way and the walker, it is a profound opportunity for meditation on and experience in apophatic spirituality.

The medieval pilgrim was instantly recognizable by his 'kit': stout staff, wide-brimmed hat, short tunic and spacious travelling cloak – which would also serve as cushion, groundsheet and rain-cover – and by his pouch or bag which, according to Gros, had three essential characteristics:

[it] had to be small (for survival was essentially ensured by faith in God), made of animal skin (a reminder of mortality), and always open, because a pilgrim is disposed to give, share, exchange.[5]

Notes

1 Frédéric Gros, *A Philosophy of Walking*, translated by John Howe (London: Verso, 2014), p. 107; emphasis original.

2 *Peace Pilgrim: Her Life and Work in Her Own Words* (Santa Fe, NM: Ocean Tree Books, 1982), p. 33, cited in Martin Robinson, *Sacred Places, Pilgrim Paths: An Anthology of Pilgrimage* (London: Fount, 1998), p. 93.

3 Jack Kerouac, *The Dharma Bums*, p. 83 in the Flamingo Modern Classics edition (London: HarperCollins, 1994).

4 Robinson, ibid., p. 127.

5 Gros, ibid., p. 110.

Liturgy

One of the most significant dangers encountered on the apophatic ascent is a tendency towards isolated individualism, which is admittedly exacerbated by many of the major themes of the tradition. Moses stands alone before the burning bush, and later has to separate himself from the 'vulgar herd' in order to ascend Sinai; the lover seeks intimacy with the beloved alone, in her mother's inner chamber (Song of Songs 3.4). All the language of interiority, and all the rather heroic language used of the rare soul who is willing to make the strenuous ascent, conspire to suggest that apophasis is not a team sport.

Sometimes it is a matter of safety. Considering the story of Jacob wrestling the angel at Jabbok Ford, we noted earlier how the apophatic disciple's willingness to deny the statements of the faith can often leave them isolated within their own community – or would do, if it knew. Investigating the role of silence in Christian history, Diarmaid MacCulloch has identified many 'Nicodemite' groups (named after Nicodemus, who in John 3.1–21 only had the courage to visit Jesus under cover of night), which have remained more or less hidden within the larger life of the Church, for their own safety; some of them simply believed or practised their faith differently from the norm of their day, while others certainly would have aligned themselves with the mystical tradition.[1]

But in the Cartesian West we tend to add an individualistic gloss to the tradition that is entirely misplaced. Plotinus' famous aphorism that 'Life is the flight of the alone to the alone' is often taken out of context. It is not quite what we mean by 'the individual' that is alone for Plotinus. In the distinctive Christian version of the apophatic tradition, further correctives apply: we have a shared identity, we are 'one body' (1 Corinthians 12.12), 'perfectly one', just as the Son and the Father are one (John 17.22). Among the layers stripped off in the apophatic ascent are conceptions of 'self'; at the height, we are so united with the God who is always the source of our being that no distinction between 'self' and 'God' is experienced. Recent theologians have done much to retrieve the significance of the ancient insistence that God is not a 'thing' but a set of relationships, and have added, even more forcefully than the ancients, that much the same can be said of us.

It behoves us, therefore, to pay careful attention to the apophatic practices rooted in our common life, the social practices. Primary among these is the Christian liturgy, which is pregnant with apophatic significance for those with 'eyes to see and ears to hear'. Liturgy, if definitions are significant, actually means 'the people's work': it is essentially a corporate activity.

We should begin by noting that for the vast majority of Christians throughout the ages, it is in the liturgy that the words or Word of God are encountered. Bible reading, the use of psalms and other Bible verses in chant and song, and biblical exposition through preaching were the means by which disciples learned the language of faith. Here, among the Christian assembly, is the material for our kataphasis; but it also includes the prompts to negation already embedded in Scripture itself, either as 'unlike likenesses', as Dionysius pointed out, or in the great apophatic texts such as the Song of Songs, or in the witness of John the Baptist and Jesus himself.

More significantly, the words of the liturgy are embedded in a broader context. Silences are woven through the words. Silences give disciples time for prayerful response, for personal wrestling and sometimes for privately 'trampling' – as the author of *The Cloud of Unknowing* would put it – on what has been said. Silence can appropriate, secure or disrupt meaning. Look up during the silence and you will usually find the gaze of Christ somewhere in the church's iconography, or maybe that of Mary or the saints, mutely asking 'What you do make of that?'

It is not only word, silence and decoration that carry holy significance in the liturgy. Apophatic authors are inclined to see liturgical gesture as more significant than words. Gestures happen in space and time but they have a different relationship to time than

175

words do. We rarely find it possible to utter, or make sense of, different words spoken at the same time, so there is always a sequence in speaking – first 'this', then 'that'; first the affirmation, *then* the negation. Within the constraints of the number of limbs available, however, we can make several gestures at the same time. We can point in different directions simultaneously. We can display a range of divine 'likenesses'. In the complex interplay of tensions and contradictions, an apophatic moment is incarnated.

Perhaps more importantly, words work through grammar, the rules that govern the construction of meaning. And grammars – at least among the cultures in which the apophatic tradition is forged – largely tend to work with 'subject' and 'object': we name the thing we're going to talk about and then we say something about it: 'The cat sat on the mat.' As we have already seen, this doesn't work at all well when what we want to talk about is no thing. Apophasis has to do violence to speech. But gesture works differently: it is about process, event, flow. Something happens but it isn't necessarily 'a thing' that has happened. We experience something but it isn't necessarily 'an experience'.

Particularly in the long eras before video cameras, gestures couldn't be 'caught' either. Waving or drowning? Blinking or winking? A gesture occurs but it is we who have the task of making sense of it. There is an obliquity in gesture that makes it a more suitable carrier of divine meaning than speech. Unlike material objects and verbal certainties, gestures are rarely the stuff of idols.

The Christian community has many liturgies, but *the* liturgy, the primary liturgy, is the Eucharist, Holy Communion. This liturgy has a shape, much like a symphony does. It builds to a climax, a zoomed-in focus on hands: the hands of the president, raising, blessing, breaking, giving. These four gestures express the whole heart of the Christian faith – from them you could learn almost everything you need to know. And the gestures flow. They don't belong to one time or place; they are not individual. They are both Christ's gestures and the priest's, gestures both here and now and timeless. At this focal point of the liturgy, speech is again fractured:

it is broken into the sort of little repeated phrases characteristic of great love or great sorrow – 'the body of Christ . . . the body of Christ . . . the body of Christ'; it is punctuated by silence and song, perhaps music and the ringing of bells; it may be passed back and forth in call and response, or it may be the work of only one voice. However it is marked, this is sacramental speech, recalling the Genesis-speech of God himself: it is speech that changes the world, speech that recreates. Only when the Word is broken, in bread and speech, can we be fed by it.

We noted earlier that taste is the most intimate of all the senses, as Hadewijch of Antwerp said: 'Love's most intimate union is through eating, tasting, and seeing interiorly.' When we think of the soul's union/communion with God 'in unknowing', it should not surprise us that this might happen during the 'people's work' in a busy church.[2] Maximus the Confessor's explanation of the eucharistic liturgy explicitly identifies liturgical 'Communion' with mystical 'union':

> The profession 'One is Holy' and what follows, which is voiced by all the people at the end of the mystical service, represents the gathering and union beyond reason and understanding which will take place between those who have been mystically and wisely initiated by God and the mysterious oneness of the divine simplicity . . . There they behold the light of the invisible and ineffable glory and become themselves together with the angels on high open to the blessed purity. After this, as the climax of everything, comes the distribution of the sacrament, which transforms into itself . . . those who worthily share in it . . . all of God entirely fills them and leaves no part of them empty of his presence.[3]

If the gestures of hands during the Eucharist are the zoomed-in focus of the liturgy, the zoomed-out wide focus alerts us to a larger-scale drama. At different times, items may be veiled and then revealed. Material symbols are displayed, processed: perhaps a cross, an icon, a Gospel-book, robes, a relic, eucharistic elements. Their very materiality enables them to function in the same way as the words Dionysius described as unlike likenesses: the mind is forced to search for the meaning that lies beyond the material image. Thus the liturgy itself familiarizes believers with the processes of 'abstraction' or 'stripping', offering an apprenticeship in the disciplines of ascent, which was made all the clearer in the early Church's practice of excluding all but the baptized from the core of the eucharistic liturgy. The spiritual geography of ascent and descent can be represented by the various parts of a church building (entrance, font, nave and sanctuary); solemn processions towards the altar signify the soul's ascent to the Cloud of meeting, passing through and beyond pulpit and lectern where the 'liturgy of the Word' is enacted; solemn processions from altar to nave or to the doors may symbolize the Incarnation, Christ's 'descent' into the world, or the believer's return to the world of action, fed and energized by the experience of Communion.

In watching or participating in these holy processions, the congregation are offered a spirituality centred on drama and activity, not substance and proposition. They are offered a tutorial in ascent, or perhaps it would be better to use Dionysius' preferred term, 'uplifting', because the ascent is not an active intellectual process of reasoned interpretation of the symbols of the liturgy. It is the presence of the Holy Spirit by grace in the worship of the Church, lifting souls towards heaven.[4]

The fourth Gospel offers no account of the 'institution of the Eucharist': the focal action at the Last Supper is Jesus' stripping off to wash his disciples' feet. Instead, the themes of bread and wine swirl through the whole Gospel, most notably in the miracle of the wine at the wedding in Cana in chapter 2, the great teachings on bread in chapter 6 and the proclamation 'I am the true vine' in chapter 15.

The other three Gospels all describe Jesus' sharing bread and wine at the Last Supper, naming it his 'body' and 'blood'. They leave us in no doubt that Jesus anticipated his imminent arrest and death. Knowing that time was short, the Teacher's mind was focused on the question of what to do to secure his teaching, how to plant the message in his followers' hearts in such a way that it could not be uprooted in the impending storm. He could have summoned a scribe and dictated a magisterial summary; he could have sat down with the 'core leadership team' for an intensive coaching session; he could have given formal instructions about a 'transition' and set out an institutional blueprint for the future Church. But Jesus did none of these things; he devoted precious time, once again, to a meal.

Our repeated liturgical re-enactment of that last meal is driven by our recognition that it was his chosen symbol for the heart of his teaching, for the kingdom of heaven itself. Its significance would take innumerable books to exhaust. It's enough here just to notice that among other things, the Gospel accounts point us towards the messy and slightly embarrassing human business of digestion. What Jesus offers his followers needs to be bitten, chewed, swallowed, broken down, according to our capacity and need, into energy and the build-ing-materials of growth, and the remnant excreted. A testament or an institutional blueprint might conceivably be received, implemented and handed on unchanged for generations – a once-for-all deposit of faith. But a meal could not: uneaten, it would stale and moulder. Eaten, it is transformed and at the same time transforms the eater. Either way, one meal is never enough – we will need to return to the table again and again. Eating is the most intimate union but it is never complete. As Gregory of Nyssa so beautifully tells us, this appetite will never be sated for long.

Stripping and feeding: two apophatic symbols lie at the heart of the Gospel accounts of Jesus' teaching. In the liturgies of baptism and Eucharist the congregation make them their own.

Notes

1 Diarmaid MacCulloch, *Silence: A Christian History* (London: Penguin, 2014), ch. 7.

2 Dionysius significantly uses the same language for 'communion' to describe both the public liturgy and the interior experience of being 'caught up' into the divine presence. For a helpful note about this, see *The Divine Names* in Colm Luibheid's translation in the Classics of Western Spirituality series, *Pseudo-Dionysius: The Complete Works* (London: SPCK, 1987), p. 70, n. 131.

3 Maximus the Confessor, *The Church's Mystagogy* 21, in the translation by George Berthold in the Classics of Western Spirituality Series, *Maximus the Confessor: Selected Writings* (New York: Paulist Press, 1985), p. 203. Dionysius had earlier made a similar point about the uniting power of the eucharistic liturgy, in *The Ecclesiastical Hierarchy* 429A–B.

4 Maximus the Confessor points out shrewdly that this is a very good reason for Christians to go to church regularly – *The Church's Mystagogy* 24; Berthold, p. 206.

Prayer 'in the Cave of the Heart'

At sixth-form college, one member of staff was famous for his monkey impersonation. It was one of the legends passed down within the student body; few claimed to have seen it themselves and they refused to give details, but all agreed he put on an extraordinary show. One lunchtime there was an intense thunderstorm. Rain hammered against roof and windows, while the sky cracked and boomed. No one wanted to go outside. Someone suggested to the teacher that this might be a good time for the monkey impression. To everyone's surprise, he agreed – 'But are you quite sure?' he asked, more than once. It started well enough: the moves, the sounds were restrained. The monkey was cute and funny. After a minute or so it began to change. The monkey leapt unpredictably from one desktop to another, only narrowly missing students and their belongings. Its chatterings became piercing, loud and angry. Its gestures were wild and intimidating. Students huddled together uneasily. Everyone noticed that the monkey, the biggest and strongest animal in the room, was between them and the door. No one was having fun.

With perfect timing, the teacher suddenly stopped and calmly left the room; it was a while before anyone moved or spoke. That teacher expressed perfectly what meditators mean when they refer to the 'monkey mind'.

Many people are wary of praying by quietening or emptying the mind; they have heard that 'If you leave the doors of the mind open, the Devil will come in and fill it.' Better to fill the mind with Jesus, by invocation of his name, by vocal prayer and song, by words and images from Scripture and Christian worship; or fill it with the Father, or the Spirit . . .

This wariness has a real basis, but the conclusion drawn, 'not to empty the mind', is a mistake. The real basis is the mind's monkey-nature. Thoughts, feelings and emotions riot inside us, repeating familiar narratives as if we had an auto-repeat button that circumstances could easily press; remorseless narratives of failure, fear, resentment, shame and so on pound away inside. There is random detritus too: advertising ear-worms, the narrative hook from the latest television drama, the oddly compulsive game; and the wearisome obsessions of daily life – the groceries we need to buy, the time we need to find for the laundry, for sick friends and family, for the taxman. When we deliberately put aside all distractions and bring our attention to bear on the mind, all this can be a horrifying discovery. No wonder we prefer to live most of our lives in a state of distraction, diverting attention from the monkey within by means of music, social media, entertainment, leisure activities, alcohol, chatter and fantasy.

All these distractions are ways of drowning out the monkey's chatter and ignoring the chaos it leaves in its wake. It's an exhausting business and rarely entirely successful. The wee small hours are often the times when we notice this most clearly. Practitioners of contemplative prayer draw a different conclusion: if we face the monkey, offering it hospitable space without allowing ourselves to be controlled by it, it will in time grow quieter (though it won't ever completely stop its racketing and jumping); and then we will discover that there is more within us than the monkey's territory. The monkey will always be with us but it will no longer block the doorway.

In the shock of encountering the monkey within, it can sometimes seem as if we have entered a cave of demons. It can be frightening, and the effects of fear are real and potentially dangerous. It can be exhilarating too, if we begin to think we have mastered the monkey – and that is perhaps even more dangerous. Generally speaking, the better we know the monkey the less frightening and the more tedious we find it. But there is no avoiding it. Maggie Ross puts it bluntly: 'if you seek silence, then you must face your demons on the way in, and never lose trust in the working of love' and goodness.'[1]

Just as a novice swimmer needs to keep within the gaze of a life-guard, so when we begin the practice of contemplative prayer we need to do it under the supervision of a spiritual director or guide who will know what to do if we get into trouble. Practising regularly with a group, and within a liturgical framework, are also helpful safeguards. And, dear reader, here is the most important 'health warning' you need to hear: if you are suffering from any kind of mental ill-health, make doubly sure you only practise contemplative prayer with a wise counsellor. There may be times when you will need to alter the practice to assist your healing.

Those on the apophatic way pray to God with hearts and minds stripped of distractions, repeatedly emptying themselves, as far as they can, of the longing that is 'a seeking of self in God', as John of the Cross put it.[2] They seek God beyond words, in silence: this involves a great deal more than merely not talking. The fullest recent account of the 'Work of Silence' is offered by Maggie Ross, who defines it as 'restoring communion with, and re-centering in, the deep mind within us', which involves 'relinquishing imaginative stereotypes and projections into the silence, and receiving back a transfigured ... perspective'.[3] Once again the apophatic way leads us to the Mount of Transfiguration, not as witnesses but as participants.

The reality of the monkey-mind is something we can all experience. The only demons we will find when we begin to pray are the ones that have made their home in us already: demons with names such as anger, self-hatred, lust, irritability, stinginess, conceit ... They will be with us whether we distract ourselves or not. But the truth is that God is always at home in us too, more deeply, more intimately; and we can trust our roots in him. As Martin Laird puts it:

Our own awareness, our own interiority, runs deeper than we realize. If we turn within and see only noise, chaos, thinking, anxiety ... then we have not seen deeply enough into the vast and expansive moors of human awareness. When the wandering, roving mind grows still, when fragmented craving grows still, when the 'heart's passions' are rapt in stillness, then is 'the mind's cessation of its kingdom', a great letting-go as a deeper dimension of the human person is revealed. From this depth God is seen to be the ground of both peace and chaos, one with ourselves and one with all the world, the ground 'in whom we live and move and have our being' (Acts 17.28).[4]

The prayer leading towards transfiguration through union with the One is integrative: it works to unite the disparate elements of the personality, as well as enabling prayerful compassion and communion with others. This is one reason why all serious commentators on the apophatic way insist that it is not a practice of seeking mystical experiences, altered states of consciousness, visions or trances; it is the much greater challenge of 'putting on the mind of Christ'. We are seeking to go far beyond the dualistic mind that separates the subject from the content of experience, which separates the 'mystical' from the everyday and the 'mystic Christian' from the shared life of the Church.

At a basic level, we need to bring mind and body together in prayer: stillness and quiet in the body is a precondition for stillness and quiet in the mind. A stable posture and an erect spine allow the nervous system to settle into a balanced state. Many forms of prayer pay close attention to the breath as a way of uniting body and mind. Simple activities such as walking or knitting also work well for many people, so long as they can be done at an even pace, without the demands of discursive thought; some people practise forms of 'body prayer', replacing verbal prayers with slow and careful gestures.

Many of us are so unused to stillness and quiet in mind and body that the transition to contemplative prayer needs careful and gentle introduction. We are not called to be brutal with ourselves. There are many familiar preparatory practices that can lead us gently towards contemplation, including *lectio divina* and other kinds of meditation on Scripture, breathing exercises, use of sacred music or icons, vocal prayers of praise and thankfulness, or immersion in activities where we tend to lose ourselves quite naturally.

Broadly speaking there are two major traditions of working with mental attention in contemplative prayer. The first uses a 'prayer word' or mantra to focus the mind; the second is a practice of bare attention. Whichever method is chosen, the point is to maintain one simple mental activity, in 'poverty of spirit'. We are not trying to think about anything, even God; we can simply trust to our roots in the divine and focus on the practice. We are not trying to fight the monkey by forbidding thought; we are just not going to respond to its antics. Every time the mind starts to jump, we gently – without self-criticism or mental commentary – bring our attention back to our practice, to the word or the simple gaze. Over and over again. Every day.

Perhaps the most significant Christian mantra is the Jesus Prayer, used primarily by Orthodox but also increasingly by Catholic, Anglican and Protestant Christians. The prayer, 'Lord Jesus Christ, son of the living God, have mercy on me, a sinner', can also be used in shorter forms if they suit us better. The Russian devotional classic *The Way of the Pilgrim* gives an inspiring account of the working of this practice. A popular recent alternative is the mantra 'Maranatha' ('Come, Lord Jesus'), recommended by the Benedictine monk John Main, founder of the World Community for Christian Meditation.

The mantra may be voiced aloud or silently breathed. Even if we start out saying it aloud, it does tend to settle on to the breath in time; when we become aware of the monkey leaping about again, we may return to vocalization for a while. We may be speaking but we are not *saying anything*, not expressing ourselves: like a class when the teacher calls the register, our words simply manifest our presence. The words come from Scripture and tradition; they are the Church's words, not our own. We simply lean into them as an aid to self-forgetfulness; we 'stay our minds' on God (Isaiah 26.3). Or truer still, they are the expression of the spirit of one who united humanity and divinity, as Main explains:

It is our conviction that the central message of the New Testament is that there is really only one prayer and that this prayer is the prayer of Christ. It is a prayer that continues in our hearts day and night. I can describe it only as the stream of love that flows constantly between Jesus and his Father. This stream of love is the Holy Spirit.[5]

The alternative to using a mantra is to focus the mind in a simple gaze of bare attention. Ross reminds us that the biblical word for this bare attention is 'beholding': it is one of the key themes of the Gospel of John, and 'arguably the most important word in the Bible, which occurs more than 1,300 times in the Hebrew and Greek'.[6] She identifies 'beholding' with 'unknowing': it is the activity of paying attention without wrangling reality into an object of experience or fitting it into a mental scheme. It is the utterly unselfconscious rapt gaze we see infants fix on buttercups and daisies, parents fix on the faces of newborns. It is passively responsive, not actively judgemental, and thus of a piece with Aristotle's *theoria* ('contemplation') and Keats' 'negative capability'. When people of no formal religious affiliation say they feel a 'spiritual presence' in a sunset or a mountainscape, they are often signalling that this receptive attention has been summoned out of them, and that in responding they were drawn into self-forgetfulness.

The practice of the mantra, or of beholding, leads us into the state of 'pure prayer', often described as an integrated prayer achieved by 'putting the mind in the heart'. Cyprian Consiglio cites the teaching of the nineteenth-century Russian luminary of the spiritual life, Theophan the Recluse. Theophan identified three levels of prayer: oral and bodily prayer; mental prayer, in which we achieve 'the union of prayerful thoughts and feelings with the mind and the heart'; and finally:

> the 'prayer of feeling', when the heart is warmed by concentration, when what has been spoken and thought is now felt, when we pass from action and thought to true feeling. We enter into the prayer of feeling when we have put the mind in the heart, or, as the Upanishads say, into the *guha*, the 'cave of the heart', the room or inner chamber of which Jesus spoke (see Matt 6:6). This is also the place of continuous prayer, unceasing prayer, where the prayer prays itself. Now it is, Theophan says, that spiritual prayer begins: 'This is the gift of the Holy Spirit praying for us, the last degree of prayer which our minds can grasp.'[7]

As Consiglio suggests, it is in 'pure prayer' that the biblical injunction to pray without ceasing (1 Thessalonians 5.17), and St Paul's understanding of prayer as the Holy Spirit speaking within us in groans too deep for words (Romans 8.26), become lived realities. The insistence that this happens within 'the cave of the heart' reminds us that we too easily separate mind from heart in our discussions of prayer. Pure prayer is not an insubstantial, attenuated and refined esoteric practice: it is what happens in the paradoxical state when a whole person is gathered and present, and yet 'nothinged', with no defences. Many writers speak of 'infused contemplation' – something graciously poured out on us, a warm, loving intimacy. St John of the Cross paraphrases Psalm 46.10: 'Learn to be empty of all things – interiorly and exteriorly – and you will behold that I am God.'[8]

Like Saint John, Eckhart and like Laird cited earlier, Ross insists that the fruit of the habit of stripping off all attachment and judgement is that everything is restored to us, no longer separated, but united in the One that is its source:

> We come to realise that in this spacious silence of beholding, the whole of creation is present and that we are given the eyes of compassion. We realise that every moment is prayer, life is prayer, and that it is our task to immerse our selves in this wellspring of silence so that our lives arise and overflow from it.[9]

The heart's 'depths' have many names, including in the Song of Songs, the 'Chamber of the Bride'; from the Gospels, the 'Inner Room'; for Eckhart, the 'ground'; for Martin Laird, the 'Silent Land'; for Consiglio, the 'Cave of the Heart'. The journey to the heart is an interior pilgrimage that has, as well as its joys and delights, its own history of wilderness-wandering, aridities and temptations, and dark nights of the senses and of the soul; after all, it is our own way of the cross, the 'annihilation' of the self. But once we are on the way, the prayer of bare attention or the prayer word acts like a rope: hand over hand we haul ourselves along it towards this spacious place, the place of meeting, and the doorway to union. As Eckhart

knew, the ground of the soul is 'bigger on the inside': it is no different from the ground of God. John Main spells it out:

> returning to our centre, discovering our own centre, is the first
> task and the first responsibility of every life that is to become
> fully human. Again, in meditation, in the discipline of it, you will
> discover from your own experience that to be at one with our
> own centre means that we are at one with every centre . . . that
> to be in our own centre is to be in God . . . In the words of Jesus,
> 'The kingdom of heaven is within you' . . . again in the vision of
> Jesus, we understand that this basic power, out of which we are
> invited to live our own lives vitally, is love . . . The invitation is
> to discover, at the centre, both energy and power, and in silence,
> in stillness, to discover in that power the peace that is beyond all
> understanding.[10]

Notes

1 Maggie Ross, *Silence: A User's Guide* (London: Darton, Longman & Todd, 2014), pp. 34–5.

2 See note 9 in the chapter 'Ascent' above.

3 Ross, *Silence*, pp. 23, 3.

4 Martin Laird, *Into the Silent Land: A Guide to the Christian Practice of Contemplation* (London: Darton, Longman & Todd, 2006), p. 23.

5 John Main, *Moment of Christ: Prayer as the Way of God's Fullness* (Norwich: Canterbury Press, 2010), p. x.

6 Ross, *Silence*, p. 159.

7 Theophan the Recluse, *The Art of Prayer* 52; cited in Cyprian Consiglio, *Prayer in the Cave of the Heart* (Collegeville, MN: Liturgical Press, 2010), p. 87.

8 *Ascent of Mount Carmel* 2.15.5, quoting Kieran Kavanaugh's translation in *John of the Cross: Selected Writings* for the Classics of Western Spirituality series (New York: Paulist Press, 1987), p. 119.

9 Maggie Ross, *Writing the Icon of the Heart: In Silence Beholding* (Abingdon: Bible Reading Fellowship, 2011), p. 42.

10 Main, *Moment of Christ*, p. 2.

Afterword

Running Towards a Stone Tomb

Paul, writing to members of the church in Galatia, cries out in despair at their inability to grasp the magnitude of the gift they have received: 'For freedom Christ has set us free; stand firm therefore, and do not submit again to a yoke of slavery' (Galatians 5.1).

We confessed as we began this exploration that the Christian tradition has contained much 'tragic loading' in our talk of God, 'more fell than anguish, hunger, or the sea!' – and, indeed, in the shameful, grievous injustice of so many actions to which our talk has led us. When we let our hearts put down roots in familiar words and images of the holy, the tendrils of slavery begin to curl around our limbs; we bow down before idols made up of rumours about God, glimpses of divinity hellishly distorted by the mirrors of our own fairground show. We read the Bible as if it were an instruction manual instead of a collection of love poems, and say our Creed as if the truth were fossilized in written words instead of flowing through and between them – as if we were to eat the menu instead of ordering from it; as if we'd rather read the 'History of Holy Encounters' than set out to meet God on the road. Augustine again: if we're comfortable with it, if we've 'got our heads around it', if we think we know what it is – *then it isn't God.*

The prophets, pioneers and pilgrims of the apophatic tradition join with Paul in reminding us of the promise of a freedom so radical that it cannot be taken in all at once but must be journeyed into. Everything we have said about stripping off, preparing for the ascent into the dark cloud, walking in the way of the cross that is death to the individual self, being prepared to go beyond God to find the hidden God beyond – all this is the expedition-briefing for the one great pilgrimage. We follow the Son of Man who had nowhere to lay his head; we follow the Spirit of Christ who will lead us *into* all truth.

Such a pilgrimage leaves us vulnerable. Jesus emptied himself and presented himself 'as a sheep before its shearers'. He placed himself, as Rowan Williams put it, 'definitively outside the system of the world's power and the language of power',[1] marking with God's cross the point on the human map where speech may tentatively begin again to represent him:

> If we are really to have our language about the transcendence – the sheer, unimaginable differentness – of God recreated, it must be by the emptying out of all we thought we knew about it, the emptying out of practically all we normally mean by greatness. No more about the lofty distance of God, the sovereignty that involves control over all circumstances; God's 'I am' can only be heard for what it really is when it has no trace of human power left to it; when it appears as something utterly different from human authority, even human liberty; when it is spoken by a captive under sentence of death.[2]

Humility is required, then. It is essential that we understand, that we develop an unlimited critical awareness of the power-claim we make when we claim to know God, to be on the side of the divine, to be able to speak holy words. Just as St Benedict's monks were enjoined to greet every stranger, every guest as 'another Christ', so we too must take seriously the possibility that the one who is weaker than us sees God more truly, shows God more clearly. This is a huge challenge for the churches, which have built their denominational identities on precisely the opposite claim. It is a significant challenge in interfaith encounter: what would it mean to worship God in our parish churches while properly acknowledging the possibility that the mosque or gurdwara up the road might know something of him that is as yet hidden to us? It is a significant social challenge: the voices of the poorest, youngest, least educated and least able are rarely heard in our churches. What might they tell us about God if we paid them attention?

The apophatic denial – *I do not know* – humbles us and leaves us vulnerable, certainly. At the same time, it can be a tool of resistance and subversion. With the author of *The Cloud of Unknowing* and St John of the Cross, we find ourselves drawn up by love of

God into a critique of 'religion'. While we recognize and honour the power and beauty of the faith we have inherited, those of us called to practise the negative way refuse to turn tradition into an idol. We confess that our tradition is deeply implicated in injustice to God's creation, and has at times betrayed and abandoned Jesus just as his first disciples did. We are called to be an Exodus people, leaving behind the land that for so long has been both our lifeline and our prison, straying through the wilderness, in order to find our home in God.

But the promise is there, in the stories of the no-thing encountered on the mountain top, the blazing unnameable presence in a bush by the way, the lover always sought and sometimes found, the Man of Sorrows who turned water into wine, who spoke God's word in the language of living and dying. It is the promise of a place once filled with death, where God says 'No' to the beastly system that once had us in its power, and bursts out in glorious life. We have the rumour of truth in our ears now, and glimpses of presence. Nothing to hold on to, but a proclamation of good news: he is risen, he is free! Love lives! Run! Come and see!

Notes

1 Rowan Williams, *Christ on Trial: How the Gospel Unsettles our Judgement* (London: Fount, 2000), p. 7.
2 Ibid.

Further Reading

On the Biblical Roots of the Apophatic Tradition

Steven D. Boyer and Christopher A. Hall's *The Mystery of God: Theology for Knowing the Unknowable* (Grand Rapids, MI: Baker Academic, 2012) includes in its Part 1 a detailed examination of the Scriptural basis for the claim that God is beyond our knowledge, as well as some material on the later theological tradition, including Gregory of Nyssa.

Richard Kearney's *The God Who May Be* (Bloomington, IN: University of Indiana Press, 2001) includes rich readings of the core apophatic Scriptures – the burning bush, the Song of Songs, the Transfiguration – as well as offering a modern 'hermeneutics of religion' in the spirit of Nicholas of Cusa.

On the Apophatic Tradition

The Classics of Western Spirituality series published by SPCK contains good editions of the works of writers mentioned here, with helpful introductions.

To explore other mystics in the apophatic tradition than those mentioned here, you might look at John 'the Scot' Eriugena, or Jan van Ruysbroek; or, in modern times, the work of Thomas Merton.

Although it has a wider focus, Olivier Clément's *The Roots of Christian Mysticism* (London: New City, 1993, translated by Theodore Berkeley, from the French *Sources*) is a treasure trove of early thought, deeply imbued with apophaticism.

For more academic treatments of the apophatic tradition, see Mark McIntosh's *Mystical Theology: The Integrity of Spirituality and Theology* (Oxford: Blackwell, 1998), Michael A. Sells' *Mystical*

Languages of Unsaying (Chicago: University of Chicago Press, 1994), and Denys Turner's *The Darkness of God: Negativity in Christian Mysticism* (Cambridge: Cambridge University Press, 1995). My own *Denying Divinity: Apophasis in the Patristic Christian and Soto Zen Buddhist Traditions* (Oxford: Oxford University Press, 2000) examines in detail the apophaticism of Dionysius, Maximus and Zen Master Dogen.

On C. S. Lewis

David C. Downing, *Into the Region of Awe: Mysticism in C. S. Lewis* (Downers Grove, IL: InterVarsity Press, 2005).

On Zen

For good examples of Christians finding encouragement on the Way from the Zen tradition, see Ruben Habito, *Be Still and Know: Zen and the Bible* (Maryknoll, NY: Orbis, 2017) and Robert Kennedy, *Zen Spirit, Christian Spirit: The Place of Zen in Christian Life* (New York: Continuum, 2007).

Brian J. Pearce's *We Walk the Path Together: Learning from Thich Nhat Hanh and Meister Eckhart* (Maryknoll, NY: Orbis, 2005) reads Meister Eckhart alongside the work of Zen Master Thich Nhat Hanh.

Steven D. Boyer and Christopher A. Hall's *The Mystery of God: Theology for Knowing the Unknowable* (Grand Rapids, MI: Baker Academic, 2012) includes in chapter 9 an assessment from an evangelical perspective of the value of non-Christian faiths, particularly when they contradict our understanding of the gospel.

On Poetry

The two great apophatic poets of the modern era are Emily Dickinson and R. S. Thomas; there are many accessible collections of their works.

Malcolm Guite, *Faith, Hope and Poetry: Theology and the Poetic Imagination* (Farnham: Ashgate, 2012), especially the masterly Introduction, 'Poetry and Transfiguration', pp. 1–30.

Mark Oakley, *The Splash of Words: Believing in Poetry* (Norwich: Canterbury Press, 2016).

Apophatic Practices

Robin Meyers' *Spiritual Defiance: Building a Beloved Community of Resistance* (New Haven, CT: Yale University Press, 2015) sets out three practices of a faith that 'undoes' us: resistance to ego, to orthodoxy and to empire. The third presents more clearly than I have done here the social and political consequences of apophasis.

The practice(s) of silence are explored by a number of recent authors. Graham Turner's *The Power of Silence: The Riches that Lie Within* (London: Bloomsbury, 2012) is a good starting point, as is Sara Maitland's *A Book of Silence* (London: Granta, 2008). Maggie Ross's *Silence: A User's Guide* (London: Darton, Longman & Todd, 2014) is a richer and more demanding treatment.

Martin Robinson's *Sacred Places, Pilgrim Paths: An Anthology of Pilgrimage* (London: Fount, 1998) is an anthology of writing on pilgrimage.

There are many excellent books about contemplative prayer. Three particular gems are Martin Laird's *A Sunlit Absence: Silence, Awareness, and Contemplation* (Oxford: Oxford University Press, 2011), Thomas Merton's classic *New Seeds of Contemplation* (New York: New Directions, 1972) and Cyprian Consiglio's *Prayer in the Cave of the Heart: The Universal Call to Contemplation* (Collegeville, MN: Liturgical Press, 2010).

Acknowledgements of Sources

Extracts are reproduced from the following publications. The author and publisher are grateful for permission to use those not included for the purposes of criticism and review.

St John of the Cross, *The Ascent of Mount Carmel*, 1.13.11, Kieran Kavanaugh (trans.), in the Classics of Western Spirituality series (New York: Paulist Press, 1987), p. 79.

St John of the Cross, 'The Dark Night', stanzas 1 and 4, in Kieran Kavanaugh (trans.), *John of the Cross: Doctor of Light and Love*, in the Crossroad Spiritual Legacy series (New York: Crossroad, 1999), pp. 29–31.

St John of the Cross, 'Stanzas Concerning an Ecstasy Experienced in High Contemplation', in Kieran Kavanaugh (ed. and trans.), *John of the Cross: Doctor of Light and Love* (New York: Crossroad, 1999), pp. 132–3.

Pseudo-Dionysius, *The Mystical Theology*, Paul Rorem (ed.) and Colm Luibheid (trans.), in the Classics of Western Spirituality series (London: SPCK, 1987).

Anna Kamienska, 'Transformation', in Grazyna Drabik and David Curzon (ed. and trans.), *Astonishments: Selected Poems of Anna Kamienska* (Orleans: Paraclete Press, 2007), used by permission of Paraclete Press. Polish text © 2007 Pawel Spiewak.

Marguerite Porete, *The Mirror of Simple Souls*, 118, Ellen Babinsky (trans.), in the Classics of Western Spirituality series (New York: Paulist Press, 1991), pp. 192–4.

Kazuaki Tanahashi, *Zen Chants* (Boston: Shambala, 2015) p. 67.

R. S. Thomas, 'Nuclear', *Collected Poems 1945–1990* (London: Phoenix, 1993), p. 317. Reproduced by permission of the Orion Publishing Group. Copyright © R. S. Thomas 1993.

Judith Wright, 'Grace', *Collected Poems 1942–85* (Sydney: Angus & Robertson, 1994), pp. 331–2; cited in William Countryman, *The Poetic Imagination: An Anglican Spiritual Tradition* (London: Darton, Longman & Todd, 1999), p. 69.

Made in United States
Orlando, FL
18 June 2022

18921378R00136